C000081497

The Which? Guide to
Financing Your Child's Future

About the author

Virginia Wallis is a freelance personal finance journalist and author of *The Which? Guide to Money* and *The Which? Guide to Insurance*. She worked as the editor of the annual *Which? Tax-Saving Guide* and as an assistant editor on *Which?* magazine. She is Contributing Editor, Finance for *Good Housekeeping* and has been a regular contributor to the award-winning personal finance section of *The Observer*.

Acknowledgements

The author and publishers would particularly like to thank Miranda Long and David Wallis, whose questions and observations inspired this book. Thanks also to all the numerous other parents whose revelations about their financial concerns helped to shape it. Many thanks too to Imogen Clout, author of *The Which? Guide to Living Together* and *The Which? Guide to Divorce*, for adding her expertise to the chapter on wills, and to Jonquil Lowe, author of many Which? books including *The Which? Guide to Planning Your Pension* and *Be Your Own Financial Adviser*, who commented on the book.

The Which? Guide to Financing Your Child's Future

 CONSUMERS' ASSOCIATION

Which? Books are commissioned by
Consumers' Association and published by
Which? Ltd, 2 Marylebone Road, London NW1 4DF
Email: books@which.net

Distributed by The Penguin Group:
Penguin Books Ltd, 80 Strand, London WC2R 0RL
First edition August 2003
Copyright © 2003 Which? Ltd

British Library Cataloguing in Publication Data
A catalogue record for this book is available from the British Library

ISBN 0 85202 938 1

No part of this publication may be reproduced or transmitted in any form or by any means,
electronically or mechanically, including photocopying, recording or any information storage
or retrieval system, without prior permission in writing from the publisher, nor be otherwise
circulated in any form of binding or cover other than that in which it is published and
without a similar condition being imposed on the subsequent purchaser. This publication is
not included under licences issued by the Copyright Agency.

For a full list of Which? books, please call 0800 252100, access our website at
www.which.net, or write to Which? Books, PO Box 44, Hertford SG14 1SH

Editorial and production: Robert Gray, Jennifer Knight, Nithya Rae
Index: Marie Lorimer
Original cover concept by Sarah Harmer
Cover photograph by EPO-Poupinet/A1 Pix

Typeset by Saxon Graphics Ltd, Derby
Printed and bound by Creative Print and Design, Wales

Contents

Introduction   7

1   Making a will   11

2   Protecting your family   21

3   Protecting your income   33

4   Bringing up children   42

5   Paying for childcare   67

6   Schooling   83

7   University   94

8   The gap year   113

9   A home of their own   121

10   Coping with the costs   128

11   A child's own money   136

12   Building up a nest egg   145

13   Giving money in trust   156

14   Tax on gifts to children   170

Addresses and websites★   181

Index   193

★ An asterisk next to the name of an organisation in the text indicates that the address or website can be found in this section.

Introduction

If financial institutions are to be believed, to avoid being a bad and financially irresponsible parent you should start a savings plan for your children from the moment they are born. After all, if you don't, how else will you be able to afford to send them to private school, buy their first car, send them round the world for their gap year, help them to get a foot on the property ladder, pay for their wedding or do any of the other things that banks and insurance companies seem to think that parents should spend their money on?

In fact, as this book shows you, the only thing that you should really worry about immediately after a child is born – or comes to live with you if you adopt – is making a will, because the financial consequences of not making one can be severe, particularly for unmarried parents (see Chapter 1).

Equally important is making sure that your children have enough to live on if you die before they become financially independent. So buying adequate life insurance – preferably before a child is born in case there are complications during pregnancy – should be a much higher priority than saving (see Chapter 2). Parents should also consider taking out income-protection insurance to protect their family's standard of living should they find themselves unable to earn because of long-term illness. This is especially important for lone parents, who do not have a partner's income to fall back on (see Chapter 3).

In the early years of a child's life at least, finding ways of coping with the extra costs – and the inevitable fall in income – that the birth of a child brings (see Chapter 10) is likely to be a higher priority than saving up for things that are a long way off. According to one mother, it wasn't until her two boys started school and she no longer had to pay for childcare that she seriously began to think about saving for their future.

That's not to say that saving for children is a bad idea but, as one mother laughingly put it when asked if she had savings plans for her children, 'Children and saving? Children and spending, more like!'.

Children and spending certainly do seem to go together. First, there's the £1,000 or so you may need to spend on essential baby kit – although one survey by American Express in March 2003 put the cost of preparing for a new baby as high as £3,500. And you can expect the ongoing costs of keeping your children fed, clothed and entertained to add an average £400 to your monthly outgoings (according to *Which?*, March 2002). However, it's not all bad news because parents get some help with these extra costs in the form of Child Benefit. In addition, an estimated nine out of ten families are eligible for additional financial help from the new Child Tax Credit, which is a means-tested top-up to Child Benefit available to tax-payers and non-taxpayers alike (see Chapter 4).

Working parents who need to pay for childcare face a yearly bill of between £5,000 and £25,000, which can be, unless they are eligible for help with costs through the Government's new Childcare Tax Credit (see Chapter 5), 'like taking out a second mortgage', as a new mother described it. For those going into the private sector, school fees can be as high as £12,000 a year, and that's not even at a board-ing school. But even parents who stay in the state sector can expect the cost of school uniform, school trips and after-school childcare to add about £2,500 a year (according to a Norwich Union survey in August 2002) to the total cost of bringing up a child (see Chapter 6). Then there's the expense of keeping children amused in the school holidays, which can be as little as £300 or as much as £3,000 (see Chapter 5). Some of these costs are unavoidable but, as this book shows, parents can plan for them carefully, and find the most bene-ficial ways of saving for their children's needs.

As savings institutions were quick to point out when the Government published its proposals for the future of further edu-cation at the beginning of 2003, the changes to tuition fees, coupled with the fact that student loans are now the mainstay of student support, mean that parents who want to put their child through a typical three-year degree course face a bill of over £20,000. Except that this isn't strictly true. The most that the Government *expects* parents to contribute to a student's expenses at university is actually only £2,360 a year (with the rest coming from the Government-backed Student Loans Company, see Chapter 7). Of this, £1,125 is for the tuition fee, but only 40 per cent of parents are asked to pay this in full. From the 2006–7 academic year, although universities will be allowed to charge anything from £0 to £3,000 for tuition, the fee will no longer have to be paid up-front at the start of the academic year because students will be able to postpone payment until after they graduate. The Government has also hinted that it is considering treating students as financially independent of their parents – as already happens for students over 25 years old – which could mean that in the future, parents will have a free choice as to whether or not they contribute to the costs of their student offspring. So much of the alarmism in the media about the cost of putting a child through university education is misplaced, and parents do not need to panic about this issue.

Getting to the point where a child is financially independent doesn't come cheap – estimates of the total cost of bringing up a child range from £80,000 to well over £250,000 if school fees and university costs are involved. The bill will be higher for parents who choose to pay for optional extras such as a gap year (see Chapter 8), and/or helping adult children to get a foot on the property ladder (see Chapter 9).

But it's not only parents who are interested in saving for their children. Grandparents – and other generous relatives – are often keen to mark the birth of a child either by giving money directly to the child (see Chapter 11), or by investing money on his or her behalf to help out with future expenses (see Chapter 12). Parents and grandparents who are concerned about keeping control over money given to children can consider setting up a trust (see Chapter 13), which can also can also have the advantage of helping to minimise a future inheritance tax bill (see Chapter 14).

If you are a parent or a grandparent worried or confused by the pressure put on you by financial institutions about doing the best for your children or grandchildren, you will find reassurance and practical advice on the essentials in this handbook. *The Which? Guide to Financing Your Child's Future* shows you what you are really up against, what sources of help you can tap into and how you can manage the costs involved.

Chapter 1

Making a will

It may seem a bit odd to start a book on financing your child's future with the rather morbid subject of death and what you would want to happen if your children were left without one or both of their parents. But if you don't address this less-than-cheery issue, you risk leaving your children to be cared for by someone you wouldn't have chosen and having the law decide who gets what of the money you leave behind.

Why you should make a will

Making a will is the only way of ensuring that you have a say in who you would like to inherit your worldly goods and who you would like to take care of money you leave to your children until they are old enough to look after it for themselves. You can also use a will to appoint guardians for your children. You should make a will – or update an existing one – and you should do it as soon after the birth of a child as possible. The same applies if you adopt or become the legal guardian of a child. Parents, whether married or unmarried, should *each* make a will. Even if you don't get round to making a

> **WARNING**
>
> Not appointing guardians can cause unnecessary upset both to your children and to other members of your close family. It is not unheard of for protracted and expensive legal battles to take place between two sets of grandparents, for example, who both firmly believe that they are the right people to look after an orphaned child.

will immediately after the birth of a child, at the very least you should appoint guardians for your children, which you can do in a separate document (see 'The bare necessities' on page 13).

Just as important as making a will in the first place is keeping it up to date after major life changes such as:

- the birth of another child
- divorce, or separation from an unmarried partner
- death of a spouse or partner
- marriage or remarriage (which invalidates an existing will)
- setting up home with a new partner
- becoming a grandparent
- the death of a parent.

CASE STUDY: Hugh and Brigitte

When their daughter Clare was born 12 years ago, Hugh and Brigitte were pretty efficient about getting both their wills updated. But they have only just got round to updating them to take account of the birth of their son Jim ten years ago. Originally, they appointed Hugh's parents as guardians. But for the new wills, they feel it is better to have their best friends and close neighbours, Ellie and Kevin, as guardians of Clare and Jim. This is because if both parents died there would be less disruption to the children's lives, since they would carry on living in a familiar area and could continue at their current schools. While they are happy to look after the children if the worst happens, Ellie and Kevin are both self-confessed finance-phobes, so Hugh's sister and a friend of Brigitte's, who is a fund manager in the City, have been appointed as trustees.

TIP

Depending on how it is drawn up, a properly drafted will can save your heirs an unnecessary inheritance tax bill – and may even mean that they pay no inheritance tax at all. For more on ways of saving inheritance tax, see page 177.

The bare necessities

You should not put off making a will, but if don't have the time or the energy to do so, you should, as a bare minimum, appoint guardians for your children. The traditional reason for appointing guardians is to ensure that if both your children are orphaned, they will be looked after by people of your choosing rather than a court's. But if you are a lone parent (or if you live with someone who is not the other natural or adoptive parent of your children), you should also consider appointing a suitable guardian to look after your children if you were no longer alive. This is particularly important if you would not want the children's other natural parent to care for them in the event of your death, or you would prefer your partner to look after them (and he or she is not the children's natural parent). If both parents have parental responsibility an appointment of guardians by the parent who dies first cannot take effect unless the other parent dies; the surviving parent will automatically have responsibility for the children.

Once you have decided who you want to be the guardians of your children – which you should think about before a child is born – and you have checked with the potential candidates that they are willing to take on the job, all you need to do is draw up a written document using the following form of wording:

In accordance with section 5 of the Children Act 1989 I appoint [insert name(s) of guardians] of [insert address(es)] to be the guardian[s] of my child[ren] [insert the child(ren)'s full name(s)].
Signed:
Name: [print your name]
Dated:

Once you have drawn up the document and signed and dated it, give a copy of it to each of the guardians you have appointed and put the original somewhere safe. To avoid ruffling the feathers of family members, it is also a good idea to let them know who you have decided will look after your children after your death, especially if they might assume that it would be them – but it's not.

Source: *The Which? Guide to Living Together.*

CASE STUDY: Monica and Peter

Monica divorced Josh – father of her two children, Andrew and Polly – when Andrew was only a toddler, and Josh has not been good at staying in contact. Two years after the divorce, Monica started to live with Peter, whom the children now look upon as their father and with whom they have a very close bond. Monica was prompted to think what would happen to Polly and Andrew if she died when she was diagnosed with breast cancer. Because Josh – who had since remarried – is their natural father, Monica was worried that the children would go to him rather than stay with Peter. On the advice of a solicitor, Monica discussed her fears with Josh, who agreed that it would be better if the children stayed with Peter. With Josh's co-operation, Monica and Peter arranged to get an order from the court giving Peter parental responsibility. She also appointed Peter as the children's guardian in her will.

What happens if you don't make a will

If you die without making a will (called dying 'intestate'), not only do you leave a financial mess for your loved ones to sort out at an upsetting time, but your family will have very little say in what happens to your estate (that is, the possessions, money, property and other assets, such as shares, that you leave when you die), because this is decided by the intestacy laws. Where your assets then go largely depends upon your marital status and where you live in the UK (see pages 15–17).

In addition, if you die intestate and leave children under 18 years old, the intestacy rules say that any money they are entitled to inherit must be held in trust for them until they become adults. There can be several problems with this:

- trusts cannot be changed once they have been set up
- the people appointed by a court to look after the trust (the trustees) will usually be your next of kin (for example, your spouse if you are married or your parents or siblings if you are not), and they may not be the most suitable people to manage your money
- because the trustees may be required to get professional advice as to how the money held in trust should be invested, charges may eat into a child's inheritance

- your child will take control of the money and property held in trust at the age of 18, which may be earlier than you might think sensible.

By contrast, if you set up the trusts for your children in your will you can say who the trustees should be and control the terms of the trust.

For more on trusts and how they can help you to keep control over money you give to a child, see Chapter 13.

What happens if you die without a will in England and Wales

Married parents inherit everything from a dead spouse, but only if the estate is valued at £125,000 or less. If the estate is valued at a higher figure than this (which is likely if you own your home), the surviving spouse inherits all the personal possessions of the dead spouse plus the first £125,000 of the value of the estate and a life interest in half the remainder (a 'life interest' broadly means the right to income from capital or, in the case of a house, the right to live in it until death). The rest of the estate is divided equally between the dead spouse's children (which does not mean just the children you have living with you – see page 16).

Cohabiting parents have no automatic rights to inherit from each other, which is why it is so important for unmarried parents (and unmarried couples who don't have children) to make a will. The intestacy rules say that on the death of an unmarried parent, the whole estate of the dead partner should be divided equally between his or her children (see page 16 for how the intestacy rules define 'children'). However, your estate will not include your house, or any other assets, if you hold them as a 'joint tenancy' with your partner; your partner will automatically inherit your share. If you hold them as 'tenants in common' your share does form part of your estate. A dead partner's half share of a joint tenancy does, however, count as part of his or her estate for the purposes of calculating inheritance tax (see Chapter 14).

Lone parents who die before their children will have the whole of their estate divided equally between their children. So making a will may be less of an issue for lone parents if this is what a will would have stated anyway. However, lone parents *do* need to make a will if they want a say in who looks after the money left for their children (see page 19) and they should also appoint guardians if they want a say in who looks after the children (see page 13).

In all cases, the intestacy laws take 'children' to mean offspring from your most recent marriage or partnership, children from any previous marriages or relationships (even if they don't live with you) and adopted children. However, it does not include stepchildren unless you have adopted or taken parental responsibility for them.

Sharing a home

There are two ways of jointly owning a home: either as 'joint tenants' or as 'tenants in common'. If you are **joint tenants**, the shares that you each hold in the home are not treated as separate (in effect, you both own the whole home). When one joint tenant dies, the other joint tenant automatically inherits the other's share. A joint tenant cannot give his or her share in a home to anyone else whether in a will or when alive.

If you own a home as **tenants in common**, you each own a distinct share of the home and your share is treated as your individual property which you can give to anyone you please. A co-owner has no automatic rights to inherit your share.

What happens if you die without a will in Northern Ireland

Married parents inherit all the personal possessions of a dead spouse as well as the first £125,000 of his or her estate, plus half of the remainder if there is one child or one third of what remains if there are two or more children. Anything left over is divided equally between the children.

Cohabiting parents do not inherit anything from a cohabiting partner if there is no will. Instead, the entire estate of the dead partner is divided equally between his or her children.

Lone parents who die before their children will have the whole of their estate divided equally between their children.

What happens if you die without a will in Scotland

Married parents have what are called 'prior rights' to inherit up to £130,000 of the value of the family home as well as furniture and personal effects up to a maximum value of £22,000 and cash up to £35,000, plus legal rights to share one third of the remaining movable estate (which doesn't include land and buildings). The remainder is divided equally between the children.

Cohabiting parents do not have any rights to inherit from a dead partner and the children get everything unless the partner who died was still married to someone else, even if he or she was estranged. In this case, the estranged spouse has the same rights as a married parent (as described above).

Lone parents who die before their children will have the whole of their estate divided equally between their children.

Creating a will after someone's death

Provided that all the people who are entitled to inherit from someone who dies intestate agree, it is possible effectively to create a will for someone after their death by drawing up a deed of variation. So long as this is done within two years of the date of death, this means that if the beneficiaries all agree that the way in which the intestacy rules divided up an estate is not what the person who died would have wanted, they can rearrange the way in which the money is distributed. However, it is possible to change the amounts distributed to a child under 18 *only* with the consent of a court. So you should not rely on the ability to create a will after death if the intestacy rules say that your children would be entitled to inherit your estate. Make your own will instead.

How to make a will

Although it is possible to draw up your own will, it is not a good idea when children are involved – especially if they are under 18 and/or you have children from a previous relationship – so it is better to use a solicitor. He or she will not only be able to advise on the kind of provision that you should make in your will for your children (and partner, if you have one), but will also be able to give advice on setting up trusts in your will. Trusts are necessary because children cannot inherit directly under a will until they are 18.

Solicitors will usually quote a fixed price for drawing up a will – which typically costs between around £75 and £100 – and most will charge less than it would normally cost to draw up two wills if you arrange for them to be done at the same time. However, if your family situation is complicated, or if you want to combine drawing up your will with advice on inheritance tax planning (see Chapter 14), you are likely to have to pay more than the typical fee. Solicitors are usually prepared to quote for the cost of drawing up a will, so always check the expected price before you go ahead. Even if you already have a solicitor, because dealing with estates is a specialist area, it could be worth using a member of the Society of Trust and Estate Practitioners★ instead. Alternatively, the Law Society★ can provide names and addresses of solicitors with the necessary expertise both in wills and trusts. You can also get the names and addresses of local solicitors from LawNet★.

Help with the cost of a will

If you are a lone parent or the parent of a disabled child, and you are drawing up a will to appoint guardians for your child or children, you may qualify for help with meeting the cost under the Legal Help system (which has replaced Legal Aid). To find out if you are eligible for help, contact the Community Legal Service*.

Before your will is drawn up

Whoever you choose to draw up a will, it is helpful – and can save both time and money – if you prepare beforehand all the information your solicitor will need. As well as deciding how you want your estate to be shared out after your death – who your beneficiaries will be and what you want to give them after your death – you also need to decide who you are going to appoint as the:

- **executors** of your will. These are the people who have the legal responsibility for sorting out your estate after your death and paying any inheritance tax that may be due. It is usual to appoint two executors and quite normal to have the main beneficiary – your spouse, for example – as one, and a friend or relative as the other. Executors do not have to be legal experts; indeed, most appoint a solicitor to deal with the legal side of being an executor, but they do need to be able to track down your will and all the paperwork to do with your estate. You need therefore to be certain that you've appointed people who are prepared to take on what can be quite an onerous task. You can appoint your solicitors to be your executors if you do not have any family or friends who you think would be up to the task, but note that the solicitors will charge fees for the task, which will come out of your estate. You can't appoint a child under 18 as executor

- **guardians** of your children if you haven't already done this (see box on page 13)
- **trustees** to look after money left in trust until your children grow up. Your trustees need not be the same people that you have appointed as guardians. In fact, it can make sense to keep the two roles separate to avoid possible conflicts of interest. There is also the more practical issue that the people who you think are best suited to caring for your children are not the best people to take decisions about what may be substantial amounts of money. However, it is quite common to ask your executors to be the trustees as well. Whoever you choose, you'll need at least two trustees.

Whoever you appoint to whatever role, you should ensure that the people you have chosen understand what is involved and are happy to take on the tasks.

WARNING

Banks, most of which offer will-writing services, will also offer to be your executors. But be warned – the charges they make for this can be high. In general, banks charge more than a solicitor would to assist your executors.

Together with you and your partner's (if appropriate) names and addresses and those of your beneficiaries and the people you have chosen to act as your executors, guardians and trustees, you will need to provide your solicitor with a list of:

- everything you own including cash, property and investments with valuations where appropriate
- all your pension arrangements
- all your outstanding debts including your mortgage
- life-insurance policies including details of the beneficiaries if they have been written in trust (see page 31) and the amounts due on death
- details of any gifts you have made in the past seven years (if applicable)
- what kind of funeral arrangements you favour – for example, cremation or burial
- the names, addresses and dates of birth of any children who are dependent on you financially but no longer live with you
- the name and address of any ex-spouses (if appropriate).

After your will is drawn up

After your will has been drawn up, for it to be valid you will need to sign it in the presence of two witnesses. Neither witness should be a beneficiary under the will nor married to any of your beneficiaries, or the gifts to them will fail. While not legally necessary, it makes sense to give copies of the will to your executors and to tell them where they can locate the original. You can keep the original at home or ask your solicitor look after it for you (there is usually no charge for this). An alternative is to file it at a District Probate Registry or Probate Sub-Registry (your nearest will be listed in the phone book), which costs £15.

Chapter 2

Protecting your family

Just as important as making a will is arranging some sort of financial provision for your children in case you die – and/or they are orphaned – before they are old enough to fend for themselves. The main way of doing this is by buying life insurance, which can help to ensure that a surviving parent would not have to suffer a drop in his or her standard of living, or that there is money for your children's guardians to use to meet the additional expenses that looking after your children will entail.

So as soon as you know that you are expecting a baby – in fact, preferably before – you should review your life-insurance needs. It may be an unpleasant thought, but arranging life insurance before the birth means that money will be available for looking after your child should the mother die in childbirth. On a less morbid note, it is sensible to arrange life cover before you become pregnant, because complications in pregnancy may mean that cover could become prohibitively expensive or could even be denied to you.

Just as important as taking out life insurance in the first place is making sure that you update the amount you are insured for in line with changes in your financial circumstances, such as taking on the additional commitment of paying school fees, for example, or moving house and committing to a bigger mortgage.

What to buy

The most suitable form of life insurance for protecting your family financially is term insurance (or, more correctly, 'term life assurance'). Term insurance is also the simplest – and cheapest – form of life insurance. You insure your life for a fixed number of years (a 'set term') –

usually between five and twenty-five years, although it can be longer – and the policy will pay out if you die within that fixed period. If you don't die during the term, you usually get nothing back, in the same way as you get nothing back if you don't claim on your house or car insurance. However, a new breed of 'cash-back' policies will pay back your premiums if you are still alive at the end of the term, although cash-back policies tend to cost twice as much as basic term insurance policies. For more on what life insurance costs, see page 27.

There are two types of term insurance policies:

- those which pay a tax-free lump sum on death
- family-income benefit policies which pay a tax-free income from death to the end of the policy term.

Family-income benefit policies tend to be cheaper than lump-sum policies because the longer you live, the less the insurer potentially has to pay out. For example, if you chose a term of 20 years and died in the fifth year, the policy would have to pay out for the remaining 15 years of the term, whereas if you died in the fifteenth year, the policy need only pay out for the five years left on the policy term. With a lump-sum policy, the insurer has to pay the full amount you are insured for irrespective of when you die within the term.

Family-income benefit policies are useful if your dependants do not want the worry of investing a large lump sum. But lump-sum policies can be more flexible if your dependants would need money for lump-sum spending as well as replacement income. However,

---

TIP

Do not automatically assume that a lump-sum payout is best. Family-income benefit policies are cheaper than lump-sum policies and can provide a guaranteed income for a fixed period of time, which investing a lump sum can't guarantee to do. Whichever type you choose, make sure that you take into account your dependants' wishes (or the wishes of your children's guardians if you are insuring to cover the expenses of looking after your children). Not everyone will relish the prospect of investing a lump sum.

---

most family-income benefit policies allow either part or all of the cover to be converted into a lump sum if this suits your family better at the time the policy pays out.

What not to buy

The alternative to taking out simple term insurance is to buy whole-life insurance, which is life insurance with an investment element. This type of policy doesn't have a fixed term so, provided you keep paying the premiums, it will pay out whenever you die. However, whole-life policies are more expensive than term policies and – because of the risks involved with the investment part of the policy – are generally considered unsuitable for the job of protecting your family financially. But they can be useful for covering a potential inheritance tax bill (see page 175).

Cover options

Although there are only two basic types of term insurance, there are different sorts of policies to choose from:

- **Level term** insurance is the most basic – and the cheapest – sort of policy, because the amount you are insured for remains the same throughout the term.
- **Increasing term** insurance costs more than level insurance, because the amount you are insured for goes up during the policy term. Cover can increase by a fixed percentage each year or be linked to the inflation rate. Alternatively, you can choose to increase cover at set intervals, for example on each anniversary of taking out the policy, or when a particular event occurs, such as the birth of another child.
- **Decreasing term** insurance is designed to run alongside a repayment mortgage. It provides a lump sum which is used to repay the mortgage if you die before it comes to an end. Because the amount you owe on a repayment mortgage goes down each year, so does the amount of cover on the insurance policy. The premiums stay the same, however, although they are cheaper than other sorts of term insurance to reflect the fact that cover reduces each year.

The different types of insurance policies available are designed to do different jobs, so, in practice, you may need a mixture of different sorts of policy: for example, a decreasing lump-sum policy to pay off your mortgage; a level lump-sum policy to pay off other debts; and a family-income benefit policy to replace income or meet additional regular expenses such as childcare. And if you are a couple, you may each need a different set of policies.

CASE STUDY: Lisa and Paul

Lisa and Paul have recently had their first baby, so life insurance is a real priority for them. As Paul is the main breadwinner, it is vital that his life is insured. But even though Lisa doesn't have an income – because she has chosen to look after their daughter, Lily, full-time – Paul would still need to cover the cost of childcare and the cost of other help that might be needed if Lisa were to die.

Lisa and Paul need to look at how their spending would be affected if either of them died. Since they rent their home, their monthly household expenditure of £1,200 would change only very slightly if Paul died. But if Lisa died, they reckon that household spending would go up to £1,800 to take account of estimated childcare costs of £600 a month. Neither Paul nor Lisa feels comfortable with the idea of using a lump sum to provide income, so they opt for a family-income benefit policy each. Although they could get away with choosing policies to cover their lives until Lily is 21, they decide to opt for 25-year terms since they plan to try for another baby in a couple of years' time. Lisa and Paul also decide to take out inflation-linked policies. This means that the amount they are insured for will go up each year – but so will the premiums.

Joint or single?

If you are a couple, it is possible to buy a joint-life policy that pays out when the first person dies. However, this isn't always the best route when you have dependent children. If one partner dies, the surviving partner may still need cover to protect the children and so would have to buy another policy. Premiums are based on your age and health at the time a policy is taken out. The surviving partner may be a lot older when new life cover is needed, or may have developed a health condition that makes cover expensive or even unavailable. It is better to buy a policy each – and this is generally no more expensive than buying a joint policy.

How much life insurance to buy?

If insurers are to be believed, you need to insure your life for the equivalent of ten, if not 15, times your gross annual salary. However, this could result in your spending far more on life insurance than is strictly necessary. It also assumes that you will automatically buy a lump-sum policy, which may not be what your dependants want.

What you really need to do is to sit down and work out how your death would affect the financial position of your dependants, or how you would be affected by losing your partner's income.

How much insurance against loss of income?

To calculate how much income would be needed after your death:

- **add up** the total amount of after-tax income that would be lost on your death – your monthly salary after all deductions (multiplied by 12 to give a yearly figure), or your annual after-tax profits if you are self-employed
- **add** to this figure the yearly amount of any new expenses that your death would bring about, such as the cost of childcare (see Chapter 5), or running a car if a company car would no longer be available
- **subtract** purely personal expenditure that would stop after your death, such as clothes, spending on leisure pursuits, personal pension contributions and life-insurance premiums. Deduct, as well, mortgage and other loan repayments if those debts would be cleared by lump-sum insurance you may already have
- **subtract** also any regular income a partner would receive after your death, such as a widow's pension or income for your children.

This calculation gives the yearly amount of income required by your dependants to preserve their current standard of living. If the figure is zero or less, you do not need to buy insurance to replace income.

The yearly figure (rounded up to the nearest £1,000) is the amount you should insure for if you decide to buy a family-income benefit policy. If you intend to buy lump-sum insurance to provide a replacement income for a fixed number of years – until your children have completed their education, for example – multiply the yearly figure by the number of years for which your dependants would need the income and round up to the nearest £1,000.

Providing an indefinite income

You may need to provide an income that will carry on being paid indefinitely, for example, for a child with special needs who will still need financial support as an adult. In such circumstances, lump-sum insurance would be more appropriate than a family-income benefit policy. To calculate the size of lump sum that will produce the required income for an indefinite number of years, you first need to make an assumption about investment returns, because the income will be provided by investing the lump-sum payout. Then divide the yearly income figure by the rate of return that best reflects your assumptions. For example, if you want an income of £8,500 a year and you think that you will be able to achieve a rate of return on the lump sum of 3 per cent after tax (which is a reasonable assumption), divide 8,500 by 0.03. This tells you that you need a lump sum of £283,333.

How much lump-sum insurance do you need?

To find out if you need to buy lump-sum insurance, and how much, you should do the following calculation:

- **add up** all the cash that your dependants would receive on your death, including any death-in-service benefits from your employer, lump sums that your pension would pay out, and the proceeds from life-insurance policies you already have (not forgetting policies in place to pay off the mortgage)
- **subtract** lump-sum expenditure that would need to be made on or after your death, such as the typical £2,000 it costs to pay for a funeral, the cost of replacing a company car (if appropriate), the amount needed to pay off any debts and/or provide a fund for emergencies or for investing in a partner's pension.

If this calculation leaves a negative figure, this is the amount of lump-sum insurance that you need. If the calculation left a surplus, this can be viewed either as capital available to provide an income, or as a useful financial cushion for your family against future emergencies.

CASE STUDY: Angela and Steve

Angela and Steve don't have enough life insurance to ensure that, if either of them died, the family would be able to carry on as normal. Angela's employer provides her with free life cover of four times her salary, but Steve, who is self-employed, has no life cover. He does, however, pay into a personal pension, so if he died Angela and the two children, Toby and Harriet, would receive the fund built up in it – but that's all.

If Steve died, Angela feels that she would like to keep on working, but would want to be flexible about her working hours and might even go part-time. If Steve's income were lost, Angela thinks she would need about £2,500 extra a month, which would allow her to reduce her working hours by about half if she needed to. But as well as extra income, Angela would also need an emergency fund and a cushion for retirement. So Steve decides to buy a family-income benefit policy to provide the income Angela needs, and a lump-sum policy to top up the lump sum that she would get from his pension.

If Angela died, Steve, who is the main earner, might have to reduce his working hours if he became sole carer – and he would also have increased childcare costs. He doesn't think Angela needs to buy a lump-sum policy because her employers would pay him a lump sum of £60,000, which is more than enough of a financial cushion. However, she does need to buy a family-income benefit policy to provide an income of £1,000 a month to cover lost income and extra childcare and to allow Steve to reduce his hours slightly.

What life insurance costs

The amount you pay for term insurance is set when you take out the policy. The cost of life insurance also depends on a number of other factors. Naturally, the larger the sum you want to be insured for and the longer the length of time for which you want the policy cover, the higher the premiums will be. There are also other main factors that influence how much life insurance will cost.

- **Age** The older you are when you take out the policy, the more it will cost for a given level of benefit.
- **Gender** Policies tend to be cheaper for women, because they have a longer life expectancy than men.
- **Health** Premiums for life insurance are calculated on the assumption that you are in good health. If you smoke or have a serious medical condition, your term insurance will usually cost more.
- **Family history** If your family has a history of serious illness or you know that you carry a gene for a hereditary condition, the price of life insurance can increase.
- **Occupation** If you have a high-risk occupation – such as deep-sea diving or working on an oil rig – you are likely to have to pay more than someone who does office-based work.
- **Leisure pursuits** If you indulge in dangerous sports, such as hang gliding or scuba diving, expect to pay more.

WARNING

Not telling the truth when you buy life insurance, or failing to disclose the fact that you have had medical problems in the past, could invalidate the policy. This means that at best the beneficiary of the policy would receive the premiums you had paid, and at worst would receive nothing on your death.

Tables 2.1 and 2.2 show what you might expect to pay for life insurance. However, life-insurance premiums change regularly and the market is fiercely competitive. For up-to-date information on companies offering the cheapest deals for lump-sum insurance, use the tables published in the personal finance pages of the national press or go to *www.moneyfacts.co.uk*. However, since not all life insurers sell direct to the public and information on family-income benefit policies is not readily available, you may get the most competitive deal by using the services of an Independent Financial Adviser (IFA), who should also be able to help work out how much cover you need (if you don't want to do the sums yourself). To find an IFA, contact the Society of Financial Advisers★. IFA Promotion★ also has advice on finding an adviser.

Table 2.1 Cost of a yearly income of £10,000 under a family-income benefit policy with a 25-year term

	Age next birthday:		
	30	35	40
Monthly premiums for men			
non-smoker	£12	£15	£22
smoker	£17	£24	£40
Monthly premiums for women			
non-smoker	£10	£12	£16
smoker	£14	£19	£28
Source: Co-operative Insurance Society, June 2003			

Critical cover

Most life policies offer the option of combining critical illness cover with life cover. This means that the policy will pay out not just death, but if you are diagnosed as having a critical condition such as cancer or a stroke. However, adding critical illness cover can push the price up quite considerably. Even if you can afford the extra cost, a better use of your money would be to buy income-protection insurance (see Chapter 3), which provides a replacement income should you be unable to earn as a result of any kind of illness.

Table 2.2 Cost of a lump sum of £100,000 under a level-term insurance policy

Age	Policy term				
	10 years	15 years	20 years	25 years	30 years
Monthly premiums for a non-smoking man					
25	£7	£8	£8	£9	£10
30	£8	£9	£9	£11	£13
35	£10	£11	£13	£15	£18
40	£13	£15	£19	£22	£27
45	£19	£24	£29	£34	£45
Monthly premiums for a man who smokes					
25	£10	£11	£12	£13	£15
30	£11	£12	£14	£16	£20
35	£15	£17	£20	£24	£31
40	£22	£27	£32	£39	£49
45	£35	£43	£53	£62	£80
Monthly premiums for a non-smoking woman					
25	£6	£6	£7	£7	£8
30	£7	£7	£8	£9	£10
35	£8	£9	£10	£12	£14
40	£11	£13	£15	£17	£20
45	£16	£19	£22	£24	£31
Monthly premiums for a woman who smokes					
25	£7	£8	£9	£10	£11
30	£9	£10	£11	£13	£16
35	£13	£14	£16	£19	£23
40	£17	£20	£24	£29	£35
45	£26	£32	£38	£44	£56
Source: *Money£acts Life & Pensions*, April 2003.					
Figures are average premiums.					

Writing a policy in trust

When you buy life insurance, you will be given the option of having the policy written in trust for the benefit of those to whom you want the money to go. This is an option you should take. Writing a policy in trust has the advantage that the insurer can pay out the policy proceeds immediately, so that your family receives the money quickly and at a time when it is most needed. Another advantage is that the proceeds of a policy written in trust do not count as part of your estate for inheritance tax purposes (see Chapter 14), which is particularly important if you are not married or you are a lone parent and the insurance payout will go straight to your children.

Writing a policy in trust is not complicated – most insurers provide standard forms for this purpose. Your partner (if you have one) should be named as the first (primary) beneficiary, and your children as second (default) beneficiaries. Your partner plus at least one other person (who does not stand to benefit from the policy) should be trustees. If you are a lone parent, your children should be the primary beneficiaries and the other trustee should be the person (or people) you have appointed as guardians (see Chapter 1).

An alternative to writing a policy in trust is to arrange for the policy to be on a 'life of another' basis. This is useful if you depend on someone financially but you are not sure that you can depend on them to have arranged life insurance – an estranged partner who is paying maintenance, for example. You can take out a policy on that person's life so that if he or she dies, you, as owner of the policy, receive the proceeds. Note that you cannot take out a life-of-another policy on just anybody's life – you must stand to lose financially if the other person dies, that is, you must have an 'insurable interest' in the other person. You are assumed to have an unlimited insurable interest in your own life and that of your spouse. When it comes to other people, your insurable interest is limited to the amount you would lose if they died. You can also take out a policy on another person's life only if that person will co-operate with you by completing the part of the application form that relates to their medical history and habits, since you cannot fill this in on their behalf.

CASE STUDY: Polly

When Polly's ex-husband, Harry, remembers, he pays her £1,000 a month in maintenance for their ten-year-old son Ben. Polly is concerned that if Harry were to die before Ben reaches 18 (when the maintenance payments will stop altogether), she will not be able to manage. Ideally, she would like to buy a policy on Harry's life, but since the divorce was acrimonious, Polly suspects that he will refuse to fill in his section of the application form. However, she can ensure that Ben's guardian, her sister Annie, is guaranteed to have enough money to pay for the costs of looking after Ben should the need arise by taking out a policy on her own life.

Chapter 3

Protecting your income

As well as making sure that your children and partner have a financial cushion against loss of income if you die (see Chapter 2), you also need to give serious thought to what would happen to your family's standard of living if you became too ill to earn or, if you are a full-time carer, illness was to prevent you from looking after your children. Suddenly losing income or having to deal with unexpected childcare bills can have a drastic effect on a family budget and can also very quickly lead to a spiral of debt.

The main way of making sure that you could maintain your standard of living is by buying insurance to replace lost income or to pay for the additional expenses that illness could bring. This can be particularly important for lone parents who do not have a partner's income to fall back on.

However, insurance to replace your income may be unnecessary if your employer provides income-protection insurance as a perk – although if you have a partner, he or she may still need to consider suitable cover if you could not manage on your income alone. And you may not need to buy insurance if your employer runs a decent sick-pay scheme, and/or you would be able to live on the income from a pension you got from retiring early due to ill health. Insurance might also be unnecessary if a fall in income due to illness meant that you became eligible to have your income topped up, or some of your childcare costs met by the Working Tax Credit (see Chapter 4).

If you do decide that you need insurance to replace earnings, you should ensure that you update the cover in line with changing circumstances such as moving jobs, an increase – or fall – in your earnings, going on maternity leave, or deciding to take a longer career break to look after children full-time.

CASE STUDY: Peter and Melanie

If Peter became too ill to do his job as a children's worker, he and his partner Melanie, who looks after baby Josiah full-time, would be able to manage on state benefits, topped up by tax credits. The total amount of benefits he could claim would actually be more than the replacement income he would receive from an income-protection policy. However, because Melanie would not be entitled to state benefits or sick pay, if she became too ill to look after Josiah, the family would struggle to pay for the childcare and help around the house that might be needed. So an income-protection policy that provides cover for a houseperson is worth considering for Melanie.

What to buy

The most suitable form of insurance for replacing income in the event of illness is income-protection insurance, which pays a monthly income in place of lost earnings. This carries on being paid until you recover, reach the maximum age given in the policy (which ranges from 50 to 65), die, or the policy ends. You can take out income-protection insurance whether you work full-time or part-time, or if you are self-employed. Most insurers also provide houseperson cover to people who do unpaid work at home. So, if you care for your children full-time, you can buy income-protection insurance to cover the cost of employing a childminder (and/or other domestic help) while you are unable to function at full strength.

There are three basic types of income-protection policies:

- **guaranteed**, which are the best sort because the insurer guarantees not to increase the premium unless you choose to increase the amount of cover
- **reviewable**, which are cheaper than guaranteed policies, but carry the risk that your premiums will go up if the insurer has had to pay out more in claims from *all* policyholders than had been anticipated (your premiums cannot be increased simply as a result of your own claims record)

- **renewable**, where premiums are guaranteed not to go up for a fixed number of years (unless you increase cover). After that set time is up, you are given the option of renewing the policy for a further fixed period, which inevitably means paying a higher premium because the insurer calculates the cost on the basis of your age when you renew – the older you are, the higher the premiums. For more on the factors that affect cost, see page 39.

You can also buy budget policies, which either put a maximum on what will be paid out or limit the number of years (typically to two or five) for which the policy will pay a replacement income. This could leave you in a difficult position should you become permanently unable to work, because you would have to find some other way of replacing income after the policy stopped paying out.

What not to buy

Income-protection insurance is not the only type of insurance that pays out if you are too ill to work. You can also buy payment-protection insurance and mortgage-payment-protection insurance that cover loan repayments if you can't work because of illness (and sometimes redundancy). However, unlike income-protection insurance, payment-protection insurance pays out for a limited period only (typically 12 months, although some mortgage-payment-protection policies extend cover to 24 months), and – with the exception of some mortgage-linked policies – does not provide cover for other household bills or any other general living expenses that you are likely to face if you can't work.

Another type of insurance that is often seen (and sold) as an alternative to income-protection insurance – but most definitely is not – is critical-illness insurance. It is quite different: first, it pays out a lump sum rather than a replacement income; second, it pays out only if you are diagnosed as suffering from one of a defined list of serious medical conditions such as some (but not all) types of cancer, heart attack and stroke. So unlike income-protection insurance, it won't provide financial help if you can't work as a result of more common medical problems such as stress and back trouble.

Cover options

Income-protection insurance will only pay you a replacement income if you become ill or suffer an accident that leaves you unable to work. But how 'unable to work' is defined depends on whether the insurer offers cover against an inability to carry out:

- your **own occupation**, which is the definition you should look for because it is the most generous, since if you are too ill to do the job you *usually* do, you'll be able to claim replacement income
- **any occupation to which you are suited**, which is not as good because it means that you might not be able to claim if you were still well enough to do another job to which you are suited 'by training, experience or education'
- **any occupation**, which is the least generous definition since you have to be able to prove that you are too ill to do *any* kind of paid work.

An alternative approach to deciding whether you are ill enough to be paid a replacement income is to measure your level of incapacity against a list of what are called 'activities of daily working'. These are activities – such as lifting and carrying and being able to hear, see or speak – that are considered necessary for work. You will typically be deemed to be sufficiently incapacitated if you can't do three of the activities on an insurer's list.

A similar approach is used when assessing claims from housepersons, except that the test for incapacity is against a list of activities of daily living, such as cooking, cleaning and shopping.

Other cover options

As well as making sure that a policy will pay claims on an 'own occupation' basis, it is also a good idea to check that a policy provides:

- **rehabilitation benefit**, which provides a reduced amount of replacement income to top up your earnings if you return to work in a reduced capacity – part-time, for example
- **proportionate benefit**, which is again a reduced amount of replacement income paid to top up earnings if you go back to work but take a different and/or lower-paid full-time job either with your existing employer or a different one

- **automatic increases in cover** (which will also mean automatic increases in premiums) to ensure that the replacement income that will be paid in the event of a claim keeps pace with either prices or earnings inflation, or rises by a fixed percentage each year, depending on which option you choose.

How much income-protection insurance to buy

The most an income-protection policy will pay out as a replacement income is typically 60 per cent of your before-tax salary if you are an employee, or 60 per cent of before-tax profits if you are self-employed. The maximum amount that can be paid to housepersons ranges from £5,000 a year to £175,000, but £15,000 a year is typical. You get only a percentage of pre-tax income, and a maximum is placed on what is paid to housepersons, for two reasons: first, the replacement income is tax-free; and second, insurers don't like people to be better off when ill than when they were working.

Whether you need to buy the maximum cover available from an income-protection policy depends on how much replacement income you really need after taking into account what other help is available in replacing your income. Table 3.1 shows the minimum you can expect in state benefits in the form of statutory sick pay (available for employees in the first 28 weeks of illness only) and incapacity benefit, which is the only form of state sick pay to which the self-employed are entitled. You can find out more about state benefits by phoning the Benefit Enquiry Line★ or by visiting the website of the Department for Work and Pensions★.

However, your employer may run a sick-pay scheme that is more generous than the state minimum – you can find out by looking in your staff handbook or by asking your boss or Human Resources Department. You should also check what you might get if you retired early through ill health.

TIP

Do not automatically insure for the maximum replacement income allowed by the insurer – only insure for the amount of replacement income you really need.

Table 3.1 Sick pay from the state

	Minimum yearly amount you will get if you are:	
	an employee	self-employed
Year 1	£3,350	£3,070
Year 2	£3,750	£3,750
Figures are for the 2003–4 tax year and do not include tax credits you might become entitled to (see Chapter 4).		

CASE STUDY: Katy

Katy, who brings up her 11-year-old son David on her own, would have to manage on state benefits and tax credits if illness stopped her earning. As a freelance trainer and consultant, 39-year-old Katy, whose earnings average around £30,000 a year, has no employer's sick pay to fall back on. After taking account of what she would expect to get from the state, Katy reckons she would need a replacement income of £15,000 a year to be able to meet her monthly outgoings if she was too ill to work. If she bought an income-protection policy that paid out one month after falling ill, it would cost her £200 a month. But if she could build up sufficient savings to tide her over for three months, say, she could buy a policy with a deferred period to match this amount of time. Doing this would bring the cost down to £115 a month.

How much replacement income?

The following will enable you to calculate how much replacement income you might need if you could not work.

- Add up all the income you would expect to receive when ill, whether from an employer or the state, and include any amounts of tax credits to which you may become entitled due to your reduced income (see Chapter 4). This gives you a figure for your income when ill.
- **Subtract** the yearly amount of income when ill from your yearly after-tax earnings (multiply the figure on your payslip by 12), or after-tax profits if you are self-employed. This gives you the figure for the income you would lose through illness.

- **Add** to this figure the amount of additional expenses you would incur through illness, such as a higher heating bill as a result of being at home all day.
- **Subtract** the amount of expenditure that would fall if you were ill, for example travel expenses. Deduct as well the yearly amount of insurance payouts you would receive to cover some types of expenditure – mortgage repayments, for example, due to a mortgage-payment-protection policy (see page 35). Also subtract any lump-sum savings you would use to tide you over during your period of illness.

This tells you how much replacement income you would need to maintain your standard of living if you were ill for a year. If the figure you end up with is zero or a minus figure, you don't need to buy insurance to replace income.

What income-protection insurance costs

Income-protection insurance policies are individually underwritten, which means that the cost is tailored to your individual circumstances. The factors that affect your premium will include the following.

- **The amount of replacement income** The higher the amount of replacement income you want to be insured for, the higher the premium.
- **Occupation** This is a key factor in determining what you will pay, because some jobs carry bigger health risks than others. Insurers generally split jobs into four occupational groups ranging from low risk to high risk. Jobs considered low risk include office jobs such as accountants and lawyers and attract the lowest premiums. Each insurer uses its own claims experience to determine the grouping of occupations, and the lists of groups are not identical. For this reason, it is worth getting several different quotes.
- **Gender** Women pay considerably more than men because statistics show that women take more time off through illness than men do.
- **Age** The older you are, the more expensive income-protection insurance becomes. This is because older people tend to have more health problems.

- **Health** It will come as no surprise to learn that this sort of insurance will cost more if you have a history of medical problems. However, once you have taken out the policy, the insurer cannot refuse to renew the policy and your premiums cannot be increased on the basis of your claims record.
- **Leisure activities** If you indulge in what insurers term 'hazardous sports', such as rock-climbing, flying light aircraft or potholing for example, your insurance will cost more.
- **Habits** Smokers generally face higher premiums, as do heavy drinkers.

The cost of income-protection insurance also depends on how long you are prepared to wait before making a claim. This is called the 'deferred period'. The longer this deferred period, the cheaper the policy. It makes sense to choose a deferred period that coincides with the amount of time you could manage without making a claim. For example, you could choose a deferred period to coincide with the length of time:

- you can expect to receive full sick pay from an employer (typically six months)
- you could survive on savings
- you could manage because your mortgage payments would be met by a mortgage-payment-protection policy.

Table 3.2 shows what you might expect to pay for income-protection insurance, but note that premiums change all the time. You can get up-to-date information on the cost of income-protection insurance from specialist publications such as *Money£acts Life & Pensions**. However, since not all income-protection insurers sell direct to the public, you may get the most competitive deal by using the services of an Independent Financial Adviser (IFA), who should also be able to help work out how much replacement income you need if you don't want to do the sums yourself. To find an IFA, contact the Society of Financial Advisers*. IFA Promotion* also has advice on finding an adviser.

Table 3.2 Cost of a yearly income of £13,000 under an income-protection policy

Age	Deferred period		
	3 months	6 months	12 months
Monthly premiums for a non-smoking man			
30	£19	£14	£13
40	£30	£24	£19
50	£48	£39	£31
Monthly premiums for a man who smokes			
30	£20	£16	£13
40	£35	£27	£22
50	£55	£45	£35
Monthly premiums for a non-smoking woman			
30	£28	£21	£17
40	£45	£35	£28
50	£72	£58	£46
Monthly premiums for a woman who smokes			
30	£32	£24	£20
40	£52	£41	£32
50	£83	£67	£53
Source: *Money£acts Life & Pensions*, April 2003.			
Figures are for a low-risk occupation.			

Chapter 4

Bringing up children

Choosing to have children is one of the most expensive financial decisions you are ever likely to make. Estimates of how much it costs to bring up a child in the first 18 years range from £80,000 for just one child to over £130,000 for a typical family with two children. And those figures are just for the basic costs of things like feeding, clothing and keeping a child entertained. Parents who go back to work after a child is born may have to pay anything from £5,000 to £20,000 a year for childcare (see Chapter 5), or face a severe drop in income if they choose to care for their children full-time. If you choose private education (see Chapter 6), estimates of the total cost rise to £250,000 – and if you plan to meet the full cost of putting a child through university (see Chapter 7 for why you might not want to do this), you can add another £20,000 or so to the total bill. However, you won't have to finance the whole cost of bringing up children because the state makes a contribution to the bill. For more on the help available to new parents, see page 43. For the financial subsidies available to help with the ongoing costs of bringing up a child, see page 46.

Start-up costs

Even if you buy only the bare essentials, and assuming you buy everything new, baby equipment will set you back around £1,000 – although the cost of preparing for a new baby has been put as high as £3,500. In the first year alone, clothes can add a further £250, while nappies will dent your budget to the tune of £700 if you use disposables, or £1,150 if you opt for a nappy laundry service.

You will also need to budget for the £75 or so that it costs to draw up a will – which is something your should do as soon as possible after your child is born (see Chapter 1) – as well as the cost of buying financial security for your family in the form of life insurance (see Chapter 2), and possibly income-protection insurance (see Chapter 3). Buying insurance to protect your family in the event of your death can add anything from £10 to £75 to your monthly outgoings, while insurance that maintains your standard of living if you are too ill to earn costs from £20 to £200.

A sure start in life

New parents who are claiming Income Support or Income-based Jobseeker's Allowance, or who are receiving payments of Working Tax Credit (see page 55), or the maximum entitlement to Child Tax Credit (see page 49) can claim a one-off Sure Start Maternity Grant of up to £500 to help with the costs of things for a new baby. It can be claimed from 11 weeks before the baby is due until three months after the baby is born. It is also available for adoptive parents, but only if the baby is less than 12 months old. To claim the grant, fill in form SF100 Sure Start available from your local Social Security office. The form can also be downloaded from the website of Department for Work and Pensions*.

Help with the costs of becoming a parent

The principal source of financial help for new parents – whether natural or adoptive – is in the form of paid time off work to look after a new baby or adopted child. What you are entitled to depends on how long you have worked for an employer and on what your employer offers in addition to the minimum laid down by law (so check your staff handbook or talk to the human resources department). You can find out exactly what you are entitled to by law by going to the Government-sponsored website for Tailored Interactive Guidance on Employment Rights (TIGER)* or by phoning the ACAS Helpline*.

In addition to paid leave, parents who have worked for an employer for at least a year and who have children under six (or under 18 if a child is disabled) may be entitled to 13 weeks of unpaid parental leave for each of their children. Parents of disabled children are allowed 18 weeks of unpaid parental leave. When parental leave, which allows both mothers and fathers to take time off to spend time with a child, can be taken and how much notice has to be given is decided by negotiation with an employer. You will find more information on parental leave in the free leaflet, PL510 *Parental Leave: A Short Guide for employers and employees*, which is available on the website of the Department of Trade and Industry★ or by phoning the DTI Publications Orderline★.

For details of the additional help that may be available for new parents, in the form of the baby element of Child Tax Credit, see page 58.

Maternity pay

Since April 2003, all new mothers are entitled to a minimum of 26 weeks of paid maternity leave. How much maternity pay you receive depends on: how much you earn; the length of time you have been working; and whether you are an employee or self-employed.

In the 2003–4 tax year, if you are an employee, you will qualify for Statutory Maternity Pay provided you satisfy the following two rules:

- you have worked for your employer for 26 weeks up to and including your qualifying week (which is the fifteenth week before the baby is due)
- you earn, on average, at least £77 a week (£4,004 a year).

Statutory Maternity Pay, which is taxable, is paid for a maximum of 26 weeks. For the first six weeks, you get 90 per cent of your earnings, then £100 a week for the remaining 20 weeks of paid ordinary maternity leave. If you qualify for Statutory Maternity Pay, you will also be eligible to take a further 26 weeks of unpaid additional maternity leave. This also applies if you do not qualify for Statutory Maternity Pay, but you satisfy the first rule above.

If you are self-employed – or you are an employee who does not qualify for Statutory Maternity Pay – you will qualify for Maternity Allowance provided:

- you have been employed or self-employed for at least 26 weeks in the 66 weeks leading up to the date the baby is due
- you earned, on average, £30 a week in any 13 weeks in the 66 weeks leading up to the date the baby is due.

How much tax-free Maternity Allowance you get depends on your earnings. If you earn:

- more than £30 but less than £77 a week, you will get the lower of either 90 per cent of your average earnings or £100 a week
- at least £77 a week, you will get a flat rate of £100 week.

If you do not qualify for either Statutory Maternity Pay or Maternity Allowance, you may be eligible to claim Incapacity Benefit (which is paid for only eight weeks), provided you have paid sufficient National Insurance contributions. If you have not, you may be able to claim other benefits – check with your benefit office.

You will find more information on Statutory Maternity Pay and Maternity Allowance in the free leaflet, N117A *A guide to maternity benefits* available from your local Social Security office or from the website of the Department for Work and Pensions.★

Paternity pay

Since April 2003, fathers who have worked for an employer for at least 26 weeks by the fifteenth week before their baby is due and who earn more than £77 a week are entitled to two weeks' Statutory Paternity Pay of £100 a week (or 90 per cent of average earnings if this is less).

You will find more information on paternity pay in the free leaflet, PL517 *Working fathers – rights to leave and pay*, which is available on the website of the Department of Trade and Industry★ or by phoning the DTI Publications Orderline★.

Adoption pay

Provided they have worked for an employer for at least 26 weeks before being newly matched with a child for adoption – and provided they earn more than £77 a week – adoptive mothers are entitled to receive Statutory Adoption Pay of £100 a week (or 90 per cent of earnings if less than £100) for 26 weeks. Statutory Adoption Pay is not available when a child is not newly matched for adoption – for example, when a step-parent adopts a stepchild. Adoptive fathers are entitled to two weeks' Statutory Paternity Pay in the same way as natural fathers.

You will find more information on paternity pay in the free leaflet, PL515 *Adoptive Parents – Rights to leave and pay*, which is available on the website of the Department of Trade and Industry★or by phoning the DTI Publications Orderline★.

> **TIP**
>
> Being on maternity, adoptive or paternity leave counts as working for the purposes of calculating entitlement to both the Working Tax Credit and the higher rate of Child Tax Credit available to working parents (see page 56). If your time off will result in a lower income, it will be worth checking whether you are eligible for a higher amount of tax credit, or whether your drop in income means that you are now eligible for tax-credit payments even if you were not previously.

Help with the costs of bringing up children

The Government is keen on children and at the start of the 2003–4 tax year, it both introduced improved rights for new parents (see page 43) and overhauled the tax and benefit system to increase financial support for parents, particularly those on low and mid-dling incomes. All parents are entitled to Child Benefit (see opposite), but you may get more than this if you are a parent and:

- your income is below a certain limit and so you qualify for the new Child Tax Credit (see page 49)
- you are a new parent and can apply for an extra amount of Child Tax Credit in the form of the baby element for parents with a child under one (see page 54)
- you have a disabled child (see page 55)
- you work and are eligible for the Working Tax Credit and/or a higher amount of the Child Tax Credit (see page 56)
- you are disabled and work (see page 60)
- you are a student who qualifies for the Parents' Learning Allowance (see page 61)
- you are unemployed (see page 49)
- you are divorced and/or no longer live with your children's other parent (see page 62)
- your husband or wife dies (see page 64)
- you act as the guardian of a child (see page 65).

Further financial help is also available in the form of free pre-school places for parents of four-year-olds and subsidies to help pay for the cost of childcare for parents who work and for student parents. For more details, see Chapter 5.

Help for all parents

Anyone who has a child living with them – which includes natural parents, adoptive parents and guardians (even if not legally appointed) – is entitled to Child Benefit. This is a flat-rate benefit paid by the Inland Revenue, usually directly to the bank account of the child's main carer, every four weeks (unless you are a lone parent or claiming benefits, in which case you can ask for Child Benefit to be paid weekly). People who contribute to the cost of looking after a child – whether the child is living with them or not – are also entitled to claim Child Benefit, provided that no one else is claiming Child Benefit for the same child and they are paying out at least as much as the amount of Child Benefit claimed for the child.

What Child Benefit is worth
In the 2003–4 tax year, Child Benefit is worth £835 a year (£64.20 every four weeks) for a first child and, for each of any other children, £560 a year (a four-weekly amount of £43). In very limited circumstances, lone parents who have been claiming Child Benefit for a child or children they have been bringing up on their own since *before* 5 July 1998 and who have started paid work (or come off certain benefits) can claim the higher Child Benefit (Lone Parent) rate. In 2003–4, this is worth £910 a year for a first child and £560 for each subsequent child. For more details, contact the Child Benefit Office★ or ask at your local Jobcentre Plus office.

When to claim
You should claim your Child Benefit as soon as possible after a child is born or comes to live with you, as claims can only be backdated by three months. If you don't get a claim pack as a matter of course – natural mothers should get one with their Bounty Pack from hospital – you can get one from your local Social Security office or by phoning the Child Benefit Office★. Alternatively, you can fill in a claim form online at the website of the Inland Revenue★.

Once you have claimed it, Child Benefit, which is tax free, carries on being paid until a child's:

- sixteenth birthday if he or she starts work then
- eighteenth birthday if he or she is registered for work or training with the Careers Service or Connexions Service (Training and Employment Agency in Northern Ireland)
- nineteenth birthday if he or she remains in full-time education and is studying up to GCE A level, AVCE or equivalent.

TIP

If you intend to look after your child (or children) full-time at home, it is very important that you are the parent who claims the Child Benefit. This is because you will automatically get 'Home Responsibilities Protection', which is a scheme that protects your entitlement to the Basic State Pension even though you are not in paid work and so not paying National Insurance. You are also entitled to Home Responsibilities Protection if you work part-time and, in the 2003–4 tax year, earn less than £4,000 a year. Since April 2002, as well as having their Basic State Pension protected, anyone who qualifies for Home Responsibilities Protection and who is looking after a child under six – or a disabled child – will also build up entitlement to the Second State Pension.

However, Home Responsibilities Protection is given only for full tax years (which run from 6 April to the following 5 April), so to qualify you must receive Child Benefit continuously for a child under 16 from the first Monday to the last Sunday in the tax year. You cannot claim it for part of a year. If you will be paying National Insurance for only part of the tax year and so won't be entitled to Home Responsibilities Protection, it could be worthwhile considering making up gaps in your National Insurance record by paying voluntary Class 3 contributions. Contact your local Benefits Agency for details or go to the Pension Guide website*.

You will find more information on Home Responsibilities Protection in the free leaflet, PM9 *State pensions for carers and parents – Your guide*, available from your local Jobcentre Plus Office, or the Pension Service*.

Help for most parents

As well as being entitled to Child Benefit, which all parents receive, the Government estimates that around nine out of ten families will also be eligible for Child Tax Credit, which replaced the Children's Tax Credit (see page 61) in April 2003. Unlike the old Children's Tax Credit, the new Child Tax Credit is available to unemployed and student parents and those who don't earn enough to pay tax as well as to tax-paying parents. Despite its name, Child Tax Credit is effectively a means-tested top-up to Child Benefit, which is paid by the Inland Revenue directly to the person who is mainly responsible for caring for the children in the family. How much you will receive – if anything – depends on:

- your household income, but excluding income – such as child maintenance payments and money you spend on pension contributions – that does not count when assessing Child Tax Credit claims (see page 51)
- how many children you have – the more children you have, the higher the amount of tax credit you might receive
- your children's ages – you can claim Child Tax Credit until 1 September following your youngest child's sixteenth birthday (eighteenth birthday if any child is in full-time education or has left school but is registered with the Careers Service or Connexions Service (Training and Employment Agency in Northern Ireland) and higher amounts are available for people who have at least one child under one in the family (see page 54)
- whether you are working – working parents get a higher rate of Child Tax Credit than parents who don't work or who are students (see page 55).

Broadly, you will be eligible for Child Tax Credit if your household income is less than £58,000 a year, or less than £66,000 if you have a child under the age of one.

Assessing your household income

When you apply for any of the tax credits available to parents, you will need to give details of your household income. However, this will not necessarily be the same figure as the total amount of money you have coming into your household. For claims in the 2003–4 tax year (the first tax year in which Child Tax Credit is available), the figures you give should be for the 2001–2 tax year. In future tax years, claims will initially be based on income received in the previous tax year – so claims in the 2004–5 tax year will initially be based on your income in the 2003-4 tax year.

The income you *must* tell the Inland Revenue about includes:

- your gross taxable income from employment (the figure on your annual P60 after taking pension contributions deducted directly from your salary into account)
- the taxable value of a company car and cash payments shown on your P11D (which you get with your P60)
- taxable profits from self-employment
- pension income from the state or a private pension
- gross taxable interest received on savings
- gross income from share dividends (add the dividend paid to the tax credit shown on the dividend voucher to find the gross amount)
- income from property you let (but not the income you get from a lodger if the total yearly amount you receive is less than £4,250 in the 2003–4 tax year)
- income you receive from a trust
- income from abroad (even if it is not paid to you in the UK).

You should also give the Revenue details of the following Social Security benefits:

- contributions-based Jobseeker's Allowance
- Incapacity Benefit paid after the first 28 weeks of being off work sick
- Widowed Mother's Allowance
- Widowed Parent's Allowance
- Widow's Pension
- Bereavement Allowance
- Invalid Care Allowance
- Industrial Death Benefit.

However, from the total of all the types of income that the Revenue needs to know about, you can deduct:

- £300 from the total of your income from savings, letting a property, pensions and income from abroad (if the total comes to less than £300, these sorts of income need not be declared)
- £100 for every week you were receiving Statutory Maternity or Adoption Pay – so if you received either for 20 weeks, you can deduct £2,000 (that is, £100 times 20) from the income you should declare to the Revenue
- the gross amount of pension contributions to a stakeholder or personal pension (to find the gross amount, divide the amount you pay to your pension provider by 0.78)
- the total amount of donations to charity that you make through the Gift Aid scheme (which allows charities to claim back from the Government tax paid on charitable donations).

Income that the Revenue does not need to know about (and so does not affect your entitlement to Child Tax Credit) includes:

- Child Benefit
- income from tax-free savings such as an Individual Savings Account (ISA)
- maintenance payments from an ex-partner for the upkeep of your children
- income your children get – from a part-time job, for example
- Maternity Allowance (which you get if you are not eligible for Statutory Maternity Pay – see page 45)
- Incapacity Benefit paid in the first 28 weeks of an illness
- payments of Working Families Tax Credit (which is what Working Tax Credit – see page 55 – replaces)
- Guardian's Allowance (see page 65)
- any other tax-free income.

What Child Tax Credit is worth to non-working parents

Table 4.1 shows the amount of tax credit you might be eligible for depending on your income and how many children you have. The amount you receive increases for each child that you are responsible for. If you have a child under one, see Table 4.2. Higher rates are available if you are responsible for a child or children with a disability (see page 55). If you are a working parent, see page 55. You can find out exactly how much you are eligible for – and also whether

Table 4.1 Child Tax Credit for non-working parents

Household income [1]	One child	Two children	Three children
£5,000	£1,990	£3,435	£4,880
£10,000	£1,990	£3,435	£4,880
£15,000	£1,335	£2,780	£4,225
£20,000	£545	£930	£2,375
£25,000	£545	£545	£545
£30,000	£545	£545	£545
£35,000	£545	£545	£545
£40,000	£545	£545	£545
£45,000	£545	£545	£545
£50,000	£545	£545	£545
£55,000	£210	£210	£210
£60,000	£0	£0	£0

Figures are for the 2003–4 tax year.

[1] See page 50 for how this is calculated.

you are eligible in the first place – by phoning the New Tax Credits Information Line★ or by using the interactive calculator on the Inland Revenue★ website. You can get specialist information on tax credits by phoning the New Tax Credits Helpline★.

As already explained, the amount of tax credit you will be awarded for the tax year 2003–4 will be based on the income you received in the 2001–2 tax year. But if your income is likely to be lower for the current tax year – your income will fall because you are going on maternity leave, for example – as soon as you have been told how much tax credit you are entitled to (based on your income for 2001–2), get in touch with your Tax Office so that they can reassess your claim in the light of the reduction in your earnings. You should also get in touch with your Tax Office if your income is likely to be more than £2,500 higher than it was in the 2001–2 tax year.

WARNING

If you fail to notify the Inland Revenue of increases in your yearly income of over £2,500, you face a fine of £300 and will have to pay back any Tax Credit that you received but to which you were not entitled.

When to claim

You should claim Child Tax Credit as soon as possible after a child is born or comes to live with you. As with Child Benefit, claims can only be backdated by three months.

CASE STUDY: Steven and Carol

Claiming the Child Tax Credit is not without its frustrations, as university lecturer Steven and his wife Carol discovered. Steven completed the tax credit application form, but was surprised that he was asked to give details of his income and that of his wife, a part-time teacher, for the previous tax year. 'This was clearly a strange thing to ask as most people in employment would, in the current year, be earning more – which, as I had had a pay rise, is what happened in my case,' says Steven. 'I got a letter telling me that my wife would be paid about £500, but that we should inform the Tax Office if our salaries had changed, which they had, so I worried that I was no longer eligible.' So Steven phoned his Tax Office, waited ages to be connected, explained his changed circumstances and assumed this would be the end of the matter. But when he got a letter confirming that he had made contact and that his entitlement had been recalculated, he was frustrated to find that no changes had been made to his salary details. He hopes that another phone call to his Tax Office has now sorted the matter out. But whatever the outcome, he did the right thing in letting his Tax Office know about his pay rise. Because it was more than £2,500, Steven could have faced a fine of £300 if he had failed to keep the Inland Revenue informed.

What Child Tax Credit is worth to non-working parents with a baby

If you have at least one child under one, you are entitled to a higher amount of Child Tax Credit. Table 4.2 shows the yearly amount of tax credit you might be eligible for if you don't work (or work fewer than 16 hours a week), or you are a student. Note that the extra baby element you receive is given per family rather than per child, so someone with twin babies, for example, gets the same amount of Child Tax Credit as a parent with a new baby and a two-year-old.

You can find out exactly how much you are eligible for – and also whether you are eligible in the first place – by phoning the New Tax Credits Information Line★ or by using the interactive calculator on the Inland Revenue★ website. You can get specialist information on tax credits by phoning the New Tax Credits Helpline★.

Table 4.2 Child Tax Credit for non-working parents with a child under one

Household income [1]	One baby	Two children	Three children
£5,000	£2,535	£3,980	£5,425
£10,000	£2,535	£3,980	£5,425
£15,000	£1,880	£3,325	£4,770
£20,000	£1,090	£1,475	£2,920
£25,000	£1,090	£1,090	£1,090
£30,000	£1,090	£1,090	£1,090
£35,000	£1,090	£1,090	£1,090
£40,000	£1,090	£1,090	£1,090
£45,000	£1,090	£1,090	£1,090
£50,000	£1,090	£1,090	£1,090
£55,000	£755	£755	£755
£60,000	£425	£425	£425
£65,000	£90	£90	£90
£70,000	£0	£0	£0

Figures are for the 2003–4 tax year.

[1] See page 50 for how this is calculated.

Extra help for parents who have a disabled child

If you are responsible for a child (or children) with a disability, you will receive a higher rate of Child Tax Credit for each disabled child if:

- you are receiving Disability Living Allowance for the child
- the child is registered blind
- the child has been taken off the blind register in the 28 weeks before you submit a claim for Child Tax Credit.

You may be entitled to an even higher amount of Child Tax Credit if you receive the Highest Care Component of Disability Living Allowance for your child. For more detailed information on the eligibility rules, contact the New Tax Credits Helpline★ or read the information on the Inland Revenue★ website.

When to claim Child Tax Credit

You should claim Child Tax Credit as soon as possible after a child is born or comes to live with you. As with Child Benefit, claims can only be backdated by three months.

WARNING

If you claim tax credits as a lone parent, but your circumstances change and you become part of a couple sharing a household – whether married or not – you must inform the Revenue within three months of your circumstances changing. If you don't, you face a fine of up to £300 and may be asked to pay back any overpayments of tax credits that may have arisen as a result of your household income going up.

Help for working parents

As well as getting Child Tax Credit, working parents can obtain extra help in the form of the Working Tax Credit, which is a tax-free payment designed primarily to top up the earnings of people on low incomes (including people without children). How much you will get – if anything – depends on:

- an assessment of your household income (which is worked out in the same way as for Child Tax Credit – see page 50)

- the number of hours you work – to be eligible, you must work a minimum of 16 hours a week, but higher amounts are available for lone parents who work more than 30 hours a week and for parents who are part of a couple who both work at least 30 hours between them (or one partner works at least 16 hours a week and the other is incapacitated).

If you are receiving Statutory Maternity, Adoption or Paternity Pay, you still count as working the number of hours you worked before you went on your leave. You also count as still working if you are off work sick and are receiving Statutory Sick Pay (or would be receiving Statutory Sick Pay were it not for the fact that you are self-employed).

Broadly, working parents – whether employed or self-employed – will receive Working Tax Credit if their household income is less than £15,000. However, even if your household income exceeds £15,000, if you are eligible for Working Tax Credit because of the number of hours you work, you may qualify for a higher amount of Child Tax Credit than a parent who is not eligible for Working Tax Credit.

Being eligible for Working Tax Credit by dint of your working hours may also entitle you to help with childcare costs in the form of the childcare element (also referred to as the Childcare Tax Credit) – see Chapter 5.

What tax credits for working parents are worth
Table 4.3 shows the combined amounts of Working and Child Tax Credit you might be eligible for if you work more than 16 hours a week (if you don't, you only qualify for the same amount of Child Tax Credit as non-working parents – see page 52). If you are a work-ing parent (or on paid maternity, paternity or adoption leave) with a child under one, see the table on page 59 (or the table on page 54 if you work fewer than 16 hours a week). For the higher amounts available to disabled parents who work, see page 60.

You can find out exactly how much you are eligible for – and also whether you are eligible in the first place – by phoning the New Tax Credits Information Line★ or by using the interactive calculator on the Inland Revenue★ website. You can get specialist information on tax credits by phoning the New Tax Credits Helpline★.

Table 4.3 Tax credits for working parents

Help for a lone parent or couple working 16–30 hours a week

Household income [1]	one child	two children	three children
£5,000	£5,015	£6,460	£7,905
£10,000	£3,185	£4,630	£6,080
£15,000	£1,335	£2,780	£4,225
£20,000	£545	£930	£2,375
£25,000	£545	£545	£545
£30,000	£545	£545	£545
£35,000	£545	£545	£545
£40,000	£545	£545	£545
£45,000	£545	£545	£545
£50,000	£545	£545	£545
£55,000	£210	£210	£210
£60,000	£0	£0	£0

Help for a lone parent or couple working more than 30 hours a week [2]

Household income [1]	one child	two children	three children
£5,000	£5,635	£7,080	£8,525
£10,000	£3,810	£5,255	£6,700
£15,000	£1,960	£3,400	£4,850
£20,000	£545	£1,550	£3,000
£25,000	£545	£545	£1,150
£30,000	£545	£545	£545
£35,000	£545	£545	£545
£40,000	£545	£545	£545
£45,000	£545	£545	£545
£50,000	£545	£545	£545
£55,000	£210	£210	£210
£60,000	£0	£0	£0

Figures are for the 2003–4 tax year.
[1] See page 50 for how this is calculated.
[2] Or you work more than 16 hours a week and your partner is incapacitated.

Off work through illness

If you are off work with a long-term illness or you can't work because you have suffered a disabling injury, you may become eligible for – or become entitled to a higher amount of – Working Tax Credit (see page 55) if your earnings have fallen as a result of being ill or injured. As well as the basic amount of Working Tax Credit, the rules say that you are eligible for the extra disability element if your recent disablement or sickness:

- puts you at a disadvantage in getting a job *and*
- is likely to last for the next six months or for the rest of your life and
- has resulted in your before-tax earnings falling by at least 20 per cent.

To be eligible for the disability element, you must also be receiving one of the following for at least 20 weeks:

- Statutory Sick Pay
- Sick Pay from an employer
- Incapacity Benefit paid at the short-term lower rate
- Income Support paid on the grounds of incapacity for work
- National Insurance Credits awarded on the grounds of incapacity for work.

For more detailed information on the eligibility rules, contact the New Tax Credits Helpline* or read the information on the Inland Revenue* website.

What tax credits are worth for working parents of a baby

Table 4.4 shows the combined amounts of Working and Child Tax Credit you might be eligible for if you are a working parent (or not working but on paid maternity, paternity or adoption leave) with at least one child under one.

You can find out exactly how much you are eligible for – and also whether you are eligible in the first place – by phoning the New Tax Credits Information Line★ or by using the interactive calculator on the Inland Revenue★ website. You can get specialist information on tax credits by phoning the New Tax Credits Helpline★.

Table 4.4 Tax credits for working parents with a child under one

Help for a lone parent or couple working 16 to 30 hours a week			
Household income [1]	one child	two children	three children
£5,000	£5,560	£7,005	£8,450
£10,000	£3,730	£5,175	£6,625
£15,000	£1,880	£3,325	£4,770
£20,000	£1,090	£1,475	£2,920
£25,000	£1,090	£1,090	£1,090
£30,000	£1,090	£1,090	£1,090
£35,000	£1,090	£1,090	£1,090
£40,000	£1,090	£1,090	£1,090
£45,000	£1,090	£1,090	£1,090
£50,000	£1,090	£1,090	£1,090
£55,000	£755	£755	£755
£60,000	£425	£425	£425
£65,000	£90	£90	£90
£70,000	£0	£0	£0
Help for a lone parent or couple working more than 30 hours a week [2]			
Household income [1]	one child	two children	three children
£5,000	£6,180	£7,625	£9,070
£10,000	£4,355	£5,800	£7,245
£15,000	£2,505	£3,950	£5,395
£20,000	£1,090	£2,100	£3,545
£25,000	£1,090	£1,090	£1,695
£30,000	£1,090	£1,090	£1,090
£35,000	£1,090	£1,090	£1,090
£40,000	£1,090	£1,090	£1,090
£45,000	£1,090	£1,090	£1,090
£50,000	£1,090	£1,090	£1,090
£55,000	£755	£755	£755
£60,000	£425	£425	£425
£65,000	£90	£90	£90
£70,000	£0	£0	£0

Figures are for the 2003–4 tax year.
[1] See page 50 for how this is calculated.
[2] Or you work more than 16 hours a week and your partner is incapacitated.

Extra help for disabled parents

Disabled parents get the same amount of Child Tax Credit as other parents, but those who work are eligible for a higher amount of Working Tax Credit through the addition of the disabled worker element. The general eligibility rules are the same as for working parents who are not disabled (see page 55). For the purposes of being eligible for the higher disabled worker element of the Working Tax Credit, you are classed as disabled if you have an illness or a disability that puts you at a disadvantage in getting a job and you currently receive one of the following benefits:

- Disability Living Allowance
- Attendance Allowance
- War Disablement Pension
- Industrial Injuries Disablement Benefit
- an invalid carriage or other vehicle provided under the Invalid Vehicle Scheme.

You may also qualify if you now have a job but have been or are still claiming:

- Incapacity Benefit
- Severe Disablement Allowance
- Income Support that includes a disability premium
- Housing Benefit that includes a disability premium
- Council Tax Benefit that includes a disability premium.

You may be able to get an even higher amount of tax credit if you (or your partner if you have one) are getting the Highest Care Component of the Disability Living Allowance or the Higher Rate of Attendance Allowance. Provided you qualify for payments of the Working Tax Credit, you will also be eligible for the severe disability element. This is also the case if you qualify for payments of the Working Tax Credit, but it is your partner who receives Disability Living Allowance or Attendance Allowance. For more detailed information on the eligibility rules, contact the New Tax Credits Helpline★ or read the information on the Inland Revenue★ website.

When to claim Working Tax Credit

Claims for both Child Tax Credit and Working Tax Credit can be backdated only three months, so working parents should claim as quickly as possible. If you increase your hours to more than either 16 or 30 a week (which qualifies you for higher amounts of tax credits), you should let the Inland Revenue know as soon as possible after you start working longer hours. You should also let the Revenue know if you reduce your hours and either are no longer eligible for Working Tax Credit, or you no longer qualify for a higher amount because you work fewer than 30 hours a week.

Children's Tax Credit

Until April 2003 – when Child Tax Credit became available – some taxpaying parents (and guardians) were able to claim the Children's Tax Credit if they had at least one child under 16 living with them at the start of the tax year. In the 2001–2 tax year, the Children's Tax Credit was worth £520, and in the 2002–3 tax year, it was worth £529 a year unless you qualified for the higher baby rate (available only in 2002–3), which was worth a yearly amount of £1,049. If a parent was a higher-rate taxpayer (or, if part of a couple, one partner was a higher-rate taxpayer), the amount given was gradually withdrawn at a rate of £1 for every £15 of income taxed at the higher rate of income tax of 40 per cent. This meant that if one parent earned over £41,735 in 2001–2 and over £42,450 in 2002–3, he or she was usually not eligible for Children's Tax Credit. If you earned less than those amounts in those tax years, and you didn't claim Children's Tax Credit, you can still put in a backdated claim – contact your Tax Office for details.

Help for student parents

As well as being able to claim Child Tax Credit for non-working parents (see page 51), full-time students with dependent children may be able to claim the Parents' Learning Allowance, which is a non-repayable grant worth up to £1,300 (in the 2003–4 academic year). How much you get depends on your income (and that of your partner if you have one). You will be eligible for the Parents'

Learning Allowance – which is meant to help with course-related costs – if you are already getting the Childcare Grant (see Chapter 5). For more information on how to claim the grants available to you, contact your Local Education Authority.

Help for parents who split up

The main source of help for the cost of bringing up children as a lone parent following the break-up of a relationship is child maintenance. If a parting couple cannot agree between them how much maintenance will be paid, then by using a solicitor and/or mediator (who help couples come to an agreement over how their finances will be arranged after a split), the parent who will be the main carer of the child(ren) can apply to the Child Support Agency★ for a maintenance assessment. (You can usually apply for child maintenance through the courts only if your ex-spouse or ex-partner lives abroad.)

To find a solicitor who can provide specialist help to couples with children who are splitting up, contact the Solicitors Family Law Association★. The Family Mediators' Association★, the UK College of Family Mediators★, Mediation Northern Ireland★ and Family Mediation Scotland★ can provide a list of mediators in your area. Alternatively, ask your solicitor for names of local mediators. For more information on applying for a maintenance assessment, call the Child Support Agency Enquiry Line★ and ask for the free leaflet, CSL101 *Child Support for parents who live apart*, which is also available from your local Jobcentre Plus office.

How child maintenance is worked out

If you apply for a maintenance assessment from the Child Support Agency★, the amount of maintenance you will receive is based on the absent (or 'non-resident') parent's net income, which is generally his or her before-tax salary minus tax, National Insurance and pension contributions. The child-support system – which was dogged with problems when it was first introduced – has been radically simplified and, since March 2003, child maintenance has been calculated in the following way. If an absent parent's net weekly income is £200 a week or more, the parent who cares for the children will get:

- 15 per cent of net income if there is one child
- 20 per cent of net income if there are two children
- 25 per cent of net income if there are three or more children.

The maximum amount of net weekly income that the Child Support Agency can use in calculating child maintenance is £2,000.

Absent parents with a net income of £100 or less (and parents on certain benefits, including Income-based Jobseeker's Allowance and Income Support) pay a flat rate of maintenance of £5 a week.

If your ex-spouse or ex-partner is supporting children in a new relationship, the figure used for net income will be reduced by:

- 15 per cent if supporting one child in a new relationship
- 20 per cent if supporting two children in a new relationship
- 25 per cent if supporting three children in a new relationship.

If you share care of a child with your ex-partner, this will be taken into account when the maintenance assessment is made. The maintenance assessment does not take account of:

- the income of the parent who mainly cares for the children
- the income of either parent's new partner (if there is one)
- housing costs
- the costs of travelling to work.

What child maintenance is worth

Table 4.5 shows how much child maintenance you can expect to get according to your ex-spouse's or ex-partner's net income (shown as a yearly figure) and the number of children you have. The most yearly maintenance you can get is:

- £15,600 if you have one child
- £20,800 if you have two children
- £26,000 if you have three or more children.

Table 4.5 Child maintenance

Net annual income	One child	Two children	Three or more children
£5,000	£260	£260	£260
£10,000	£1,500	£2,000	£2,500
£15,000	£2,250	£3,000	£3,750
£20,000	£3,000	£4,000	£5,000
£25,000	£3,750	£5,000	£6,250
£30,000	£4,500	£6,000	£7,500
£35,000	£5,250	£7,000	£8,750
£40,000	£6,000	£8,000	£10,000
£45,000	£6,750	£9,000	£11,250
£50,000	£7,500	£10,000	£12,500

TIP

If you were claiming tax credits before the split, you are obliged to tell the Revenue about the change in your circumstances – you face a fine of up to £300 if you don't do so within three months of your circumstances changing. However, keeping the Revenue informed should work to your advantage because the changes to your income may mean that you are entitled to claim a higher amount of tax credits. A change in circumstances may also mean that you are entitled to tax credits to which you were previously not entitled. This is likely to be the case if a large part of your income is child maintenance, because child maintenance does not count as income when assessing eligibility to tax credits.

Help for bereaved parents

There is no specific help for a surviving partner if an unmarried partner dies, which is one of the reasons why unmarried parents should check that they have adequate life insurance (see Chapter 2). But if your husband or wife dies – and depending on his or her National Insurance record at the date of death – you may be entitled to:

- **Bereavement Payment**, which is a one-off payment of up to £2,000 (in 2003–4) paid to a surviving spouse provided he or she is under state pension age (currently 65 for men and 60 for women) or is over state pension age and the dead spouse was not eligible for a state pension based on his or her National Insurance record
- **Widowed Parent's Allowance**, which is a regular payment of up to £77.45 a week (in 2003–4) paid for up to one year to a surviving spouse who is bringing up dependent children or is pregnant with a dead husband's child
- **Bereavement Allowance**, which is paid at the same rate as Widowed Parent's Allowance to a widow or widower aged over 45 and under 65 who is not bringing up dependent children.

You should claim both Bereavement Payment and Widowed Parent's Allowance (or Bereavement Allowance) as soon after the death of a spouse as possible, otherwise you may lose benefit to which you are entitled. To claim, contact your local Jobcentre Plus office or download the claim forms from the website of the Department for Work and Pensions★. If your income falls as the result of a spouse's death, you should also check your eligibility for Child Tax Credit (see page 49) and Working Tax Credit (see page 55).

CASE STUDY: Anna

Anna – divorced mother of ten-year-old Phoebe – has not managed to find work in her specialist area of fashion and textiles, so she does occasional office work to supplement the £1,500 a month that her ex-husband pays her in maintenance for Phoebe. She doesn't work sufficiently long hours to qualify for the Working Tax Credit, but because her earnings from temping are only £7,500 a year she qualifies for the full amount of the Child Tax Credit of £1,990.

Help for guardians

In addition to the Child Benefit (see page 47) and Child Tax Credit (see page 49) that guardians can claim for the children they look after, guardians can also claim Guardian's Allowance which, in

2003–4, is worth £11.55 a week for each child. You do not have to be a child's legal guardian, but you must be claiming the Child Benefit for that child. You can claim Guardian's Allowance (which does not count as income when assessing tax credit claims) if you are bringing up a child and:

- both the child's natural parents are dead
- one parent is dead and the other cannot be traced
- you are not getting maintenance from the ex-partner of a child's dead parent
- the child's mother is dead and the father of the child is not known
- one of the child's parents is dead and the other is in prison or in a mental hospital.

To claim Guardian's Allowance, fill in form BG1 available from the Guardian's Allowance Unit*. You can also download the form from the website of the Department for Work and Pensions*.

Help for temporary parents

New rules which came into force in April 2003 mean that people engaged by local authorities to provide foster care will no longer be taxed on all the income they receive for fostering. In the 2003–4 tax year, foster carers are given an individual limit for income that will be exempt from tax. The limit is made up of:

- a fixed amount of £10,000 for each foster home
- an additional amount of £200 for each week that foster care is given to a child under 11, and £250 a week for each week that a child over 11 is cared for.

If a foster carer's income from fostering is below the limit, he or she will have no tax to pay. If it is over the individual limit, tax will be paid only on the amount of income over the limit. Alternatively, a foster carer can choose to use the normal tax rules for self-employed people to work out how much tax is due.

Chapter 5

Paying for childcare

Unless you plan to look after your children full-time – or have a willing relative or friend who will look after them for free – one of the biggest costs you face when going back to work is the bill for childcare. According to a survey published early in 2003 by the national childcare charity, Daycare Trust★, the average cost of a full-time nursery place for a child under two was more than £6,650 a year, while the most expensive cost over £15,000 a year. Parents of school-age children who cannot fit their work around school hours (see page 75), and so need to pay for after-school care and care in the school holidays, face an average childcare bill of around £1,675 a year.

Cost of childcare outside the home

Table 5.1 shows the typical yearly childcare costs in England for a full-time day nursery or childminding place for a pre-school-age child. For the cost of childcare for a school-age child, see Table 5.2.

If your child is over two and you're lucky enough to have access to a state nursery school (which is different from a day nursery in that nursery schools don't accept children under two), you will not have to pay for childcare because if a nursery school is part of the state education system, it is free. However, nursery schools that are privately run can cost from £2,700 to £3,900 a year. With either type of nursery school, if you need full-time childcare, you'll have to pay for other childcare arrangements in the holidays, which will add an average of £2,240 to your yearly childcare bill.

Table 5.1 Typical yearly costs of pre-school childcare

Region	Child under 2		Child over 2	
	Day nursery	**Childminder**	**Day nursery**	**Childminder**
East England	£7,640	£7,330	£7,070	£7,170
East Midlands	£5,460	£5,670	£5,410	£5,670
London (inner)	£8,730	£7,230	£7,900	£7,330
London (outer)	£8,010	£7,170	£7,070	£6,810
North-East	£5,820	£5,610	£5,560	£5,870
North-West	£5,560	£4,830	£5,250	£4,830
South-East	£8,370	£6,910	£7,750	£6,810
South-West	£5,770	£6,080	£5,350	£5,820
West Midlands	£5,410	£4,890	£5,250	£4,780
Yorkshire & Humberside	£5,770	£5,560	£5,560	£5,560
Source: Daycare Trust*, 2003.				

Table 5.2 shows the typical cost of an after-school club used for 15 hours a week for 39 weeks of the year, as well as the typical cost of paying for a summer playscheme for six weeks. Holiday playschemes cost on average around £60 a week but, according to the Daycare Trust*, some can cost as much as £140 a week, which would mean a bill of £840 for a six-week period.

Table 5.2 Typical yearly costs of childcare for school-age children

Region	After-school club	Holiday playscheme
East England	£1,870	£350
East Midlands	£1,365	£365
London (inner)	£1,170	£310
London (outer)	£1,170	£360
North-East	£1,480	£311
North-West	£1,170	£354
South-East	£1,445	£365
South-West	£1,325	£350
West Midlands	£1,250	£345
Yorkshire & Humberside	£900	£400
Source: Daycare Trust*, 2003.		

CASE STUDY: Helena

Helena found going back to work after the birth of her daughter Laura a guilt-ridden experience. But she was lucky enough to get Laura a place at the on-site nursery at the large hospital where she is training to be a consultant registrar, so she can at least pop in to see her daughter during the day. However, if it weren't for the fact that she and her husband Ryan are both earning, she would find it very hard to pay her £500-a-month childcare bill, which Helena describes as being 'like taking out a second mortgage'.

Cost of childcare at home

Parents who choose to employ a nanny rather than make use of childcare outside the home typically face a yearly bill of between £14,000 and £25,000, depending on where in the country they live (see Table 5.3) and how well-qualified the nanny is. For more on the financial implications of employing a nanny, see page 79.

Taking on an au pair is much cheaper than employing a nanny, since you only need to pay between £50 and £75 a week. For more on taking on an au pair, see page 82.

Table 5.3 Typical yearly cost of employing a nanny

	Daily nannies	Live-in nannies
London	£25,000	£18,000
Other cities and towns	£16,300	£14,000
Source: *Nursery World*, January 2003.		

TIP

You can reduce the cost of employing a nanny by sharing one with another family. The National Childbirth Trust* can provide details of local branches that have a nanny-share register.

Help with childcare costs

The real sting of childcare costs is that they have to be paid for out of your after-tax salary. But financial help is available and you may not need to meet the *full* cost yourself if you are a parent and:

- have a child over four (see below)
- work and are eligible for state help through the Childcare Tax Credit (see page 71)
- work for an employer who provides help with childcare costs or provides a subsidised nursery (see page 75)
- you are disabled and work (see page 76)
- you are a student (see page 77)
- you are unemployed (see page 79).

Help for parents of four-year-olds

All parents with four-year-old children are entitled to a free part-time pre-school place under the Nursery Education Grant Scheme (also known as the Early Years' Grant). The grant is worth over £1,200 and is paid directly to the provider of the pre-school place. For each four-year-old, the grant pays for a maximum of five two-and-a-half-hour sessions per week for 33 weeks of the year (i.e. three terms of 11 weeks).

If parents want more sessions than are covered by the cost of the grant, they must pay whatever fees are required to top up the provision, either with the provider of the free place, if this is possible, or elsewhere. No more than two sessions may be combined in one day. You do not have to take up all the sessions, but you cannot carry forward unused sessions to another week. You can use your free sessions with a selection of different providers up to the maximum amount of five two-and-a-half-hour sessions per week.

You can make use of the free part-time early education place with any registered provider. ChildcareLink★ can give details of your local Children's Information Service (CIS), which will provide a list of registered childcare in your area. The types of pre-school provision eligible for the grant include:

- reception or nursery classes
- nursery schools

- private day nurseries
- pre-school playgroups
- childminders who work as a group.

The earliest you can start to make use of the free sessions depends on when your child's fourth birthday falls. If it is between:

- September and December, your child can start the following January
- January and March, your child can start the following summer term
- April and August, your child can start the following September.

When you first enrol your child at your chosen provider, you will be asked to produce his or her birth certificate (copies are not acceptable), and must complete a form saying how many sessions you want your child to attend. To prevent possible abuse of the system, you will be required to sign a declaration each term that you are not receiving a grant for more than five sessions a week. You must also confirm at the beginning of each term whether your child is included in the school's claim for that term.

Free places for three-year-olds

From April 2004, the Nursery Education Grant Scheme will be extended to cover three-year-olds. The structure and type of provision is much the same as that for four-year-olds, except that there won't be places in reception classes, as these are considered inappropriate for three-year-olds.

State help for working parents

Working parents can get help with childcare costs through the Childcare Tax Credit (also referred to as the childcare element of the Working Tax Credit – see Chapter 4), which is paid both to employees and the self-employed, directly into the bank account of the main carer (typically the mother).

If you are eligible for Childcare Tax Credit in the 2003–4 tax year, the state will pay up to 70 per cent of childcare costs up to a maximum of £135 a week if you have one child and £200 a week if you have two or more children. So even if you spend more than the maximum for the number of children you have, the most help you will receive is £94.50 a week if you have one child and £140 for two or more. If your actual childcare costs are lower than the maximum weekly figures, you will only receive 70 per cent of the amount you actually pay. So if you pay a childminder £90 a week to look after your only child, the most you will get is £63 a week (that is, 70 per cent of £90).

Are you eligible for help?

To be eligible to apply for Childcare Tax Credit, you must be working at least 16 hours a week if you are a lone parent, or both working at least 16 hours a week if you are a couple. Couples are also eligible if one partner works at least 16 hours a week and the other does not work but is disabled and receives a disability benefit. Otherwise, couples where only one partner works – whatever the hours – are not eligible for Childcare Tax Credit.

You must also be paying for registered or approved childcare for at least one child under 15 (or under 17 if he or she has learning difficulties or is registered as having special educational needs). Registered and approved childcare includes:

- a childminder, nursery or play scheme registered with OFSTED★
- an out-of-hours club on school premises run either by the school or by the Local Authority or approved under a quality assurance scheme such as that run by the Kids' Club Network★
- a childcare scheme run on Government property
- any other childcare scheme run by a provider approved by the Local Authority.

ChildcareLink★ can give details of your local Children's Information Service (CIS), which will provide a list of registered childcare in your area.

Since April 2003, parents who use approved childcare – such as a registered childminder – in their own homes are eligible to apply for the Childcare Tax Credit under the Home Childcarers scheme. Before April 2003, only parents using approved childcare outside the home were eligible for help. This change aims particularly to help parents who would benefit from home-based care, such as those with disabled children or those who work unconventional hours. More information about the Home Childcarers scheme is available from the Department for Education and Skills★.

You won't qualify for state help with childcare costs if you employ a nanny or an au pair unless the person you employ has the necessary qualifications and skills to register as a childminder with OFSTED★ and has done so.

TIP

If you pay a friend, relative or nanny to look after your child(ren), you won't get help with childcare costs unless he or she is a registered childminder. So if you would otherwise be eligible for the Childcare Tax Credit, encourage the carer of your child to register. You can get advice on becoming a childminder from the National Childminding Association★. For some strange reason, you will not get help with childcare costs if your child's carer – even though registered – is a relative and he or she cares for your child in your home.

How much will you get?
Although you may be eligible to apply for the Childcare Tax Credit, you won't necessarily qualify for help with childcare costs because the amount you get – assuming you get any at all – depends on your household income (excluding things like maintenance payments for children; see page 51 for a full list of the income that does not count when assessing applications for tax credits). But, broadly, you are unlikely to get help with childcare costs if you have one child and a household income of over £30,000, or more than about £35,000 if you are paying for childcare for two or more children. Table 5.4 shows how much help with childcare costs you might receive if your household income is lower than those thresholds.

You can find out exactly how much you are eligible for – and also whether you are eligible in the first place – by phoning the New Tax Credits Information Line★, or by using the interactive calculator on the New Tax Credits website★. For more on the other tax credits (and the rules that relate to them) available both for working and non-working parents, see Chapter 4. You can get specialist information on tax credits by phoning the New Tax Credits Helpline★.

Table 5.4 What the Childcare Tax Credit is worth in 2003–4

Household income	Maximum help available if you are:					
	a lone parent and you work 16 to 30 hours a week		a lone parent and you work more than 30 hours a week		part of a couple and you both work at least 16 hours a week [1]	
	one child	two or more children	one child	two or more children	one child	two or more children
£5,000	£4,915	£7,280	£4,915	£7,280	£4,915	£7,280
£10,000	£4,915	£7,280	£4,915	£7,280	£4,915	£7,280
£15,000	£4,260	£6,625	£4,880	£7,245	£4,880	£7,245
£20,000	£2,410	£4,775	£3,030	£5,395	£3,030	£5,395
£25,000	£560	£2,925	£1,180	£3,545	£1,180	£3,545
£30,000	£0	£1,075	£0	£1,695	£0	£1,695
£35,000	£0	£0	£0	£0	£0	£0

[1] Or you work more than 16 hours a week and your partner is incapacitated. The figures assume that you pay £135 a week or more for childcare for one child and that your total childcare bill if you have two or more children is £200 or more a week.

If you do qualify to have some of your childcare costs paid for, the Childcare Tax Credit carries on being paid:

- *either* until you stop qualifying for it
- *or* until the first September following your child's fifteenth birthday (sixteenth birthday if your child is blind or you receive Disability Living Allowance as a result of your child's disability).

When to claim

You should apply for help with childcare costs as soon as possible after you start to incur them. As with other tax credits (see Chapter 4), claims can only be backdated by three months. If your average weekly childcare costs rise by more than £10 a week for four weeks in a row – which they might if you pay for care in the school holidays, for example – tell your Tax Office so that they can increase the amount of tax credit to which you are entitled. Guidance on working out your average weekly childcare costs is given in the free leaflet, WTC5 *Child Tax Credit and Working Tax Credit*, available on the Inland Revenue★ website or by phoning the Self Assessment Orderline★.

WARNING

If you stop paying childcare costs or they fall by more than £10 for four weeks in a row, you must let your Tax Office know as soon as possible after the change. If you fail to do this, you could face a fine of up to £300 and may have to repay any overpayments of tax credit.

Flexible working

Even if you don't qualify for help with paying for childcare in the form of the Childcare Tax Credit, you may be able to reduce your childcare bill by using the new rights to flexible working that were introduced for parents in April 2003. Under the new laws, working parents with children under 6 – or a disabled child under 18 – have the right to ask their employer to consider requests to work flexibly. This means that you can ask to:

- change the hours you work
- change the times when you work
- go part-time
- work from home.

The right to flexible working is in addition to the right to emergency time off (see page 76) and the right to parental leave (see Chapter 4). For more information on flexible working, go to the Tailored Interactive Guidance on Employment Rights* or phone the ACAS Helpline*.

Help from employers

One in ten employers provides some help with childcare in the form of extra cash, childcare vouchers or a subsidised nursery. However, currently you have to pay tax on the financial benefit stemming from all forms of employer help with childcare, except for the benefit of a free or subsidised place at a nursery so long as it is run (either wholly or in part) by your employer. At the time of writing, the Government was consulting on extending the tax-free status of employer-run nurseries to all kinds of financial help, up to a limit of £50 a week.

For information on workplace nurseries, together with advice on how to get one started, contact the Daycare Trust*, which produces a free fact sheet.

Your right to emergency time off

If your source of childcare lets you down, the law says that your employer must allow you time off to sort out the problem. However, your employer does not have to pay you for this sort of emergency time off.

Help for disabled parents

Help with childcare costs is available for disabled parents in the form of the Childcare Tax Credit. The general eligibility rules are the same as for working parents who are not disabled (see page 72). For the purposes of the Childcare Tax Credit, you are classed as disabled if you have an illness or a disability that puts you at a disadvantage in getting a job and you currently receive one of the following:

- Disability Living Allowance
- Attendance Allowance
- War Disablement Pension
- Industrial Injuries Disablement Benefit
- an invalid carriage or other vehicle provided under the Invalid Vehicle Scheme.

Table 5.5 shows the amount of state help with childcare costs to which you might be entitled. Higher amounts are available for severely disabled working parents.

Table 5.5 What the Childcare Tax Credit is worth to disabled parents who work

Household income	Maximum help available if you are:					
	a lone parent and you work 16 to 30 hours a week		a lone parent and you work more than 30 hours a week		part of a couple and you both work at least 16 hours a week [1]	
	one child	two or more children	one child	two or more children	one child	two or more children
£5,000	£4,915	£7,280	£4,915	£7,280	£4,915	£7,280
£10,000	£4,915	£7,280	£4,915	£7,280	£4,915	£7,280
£15,000	£4,915	£7,280	£4,915	£7,280	£4,915	£7,280
£20,000	£4,450	£6,815	£4,915	£7,280	£4,915	£7,280
£25,000	£2,600	£4,965	£3,220	£5,590	£3,220	£5,590
£30,000	£750	£3,115	£1,370	£3,740	£1,370	£3,740
£35,000	£0	£1,265	£0	£1,890	£0	£1,890
£40,000	£0	£0	£0	£0	£0	£0

[1] Or you work more than 16 hours a week and your partner is incapacitated and unable to work. The figures assume that you pay £135 a week or more for childcare for one child and that your total childcare bill if you have two or more children is £200 or more a week.

You can find out exactly how much you are eligible for – and also whether you are eligible in the first place – by phoning the New Tax Credits Response Line★, or by using the interactive calculator on the New Tax Credits website★. For more on the other tax credits (and the rules that relate to them) available both for working and non-working parents, see Chapter 4. You can get specialist information on tax credits by phoning the New Tax Credits Helpline★.

Help for student parents

If you are a student parent on a low income who has to pay for childcare – and do not qualify for the Childcare Tax Credit (see page 71) – you can apply for a Childcare Grant (unlike the student loan, this does not have to be repaid) from your Local Education Authority. Students are eligible if they have a child or children under 15 (17 if a child has learning difficulties or is registered as having special educational needs) and are on a low income. This is likely to be the case if a student is:

- a lone parent
- married to another student
- has a spouse (which, if the student is over 25, includes a cohabiting partner) who is on a low income or unable to work because of a disability.

Are you eligible for help?

The Childcare Grant is means-tested, so how much you get depends on your household income. If you make use of a free part-time childcare place under the Nursery Education Grant Scheme (see page 70), this is taken into account. In addition to the means test, in order to qualify for the grant you must be a full-time student with dependent children in childcare with a provider who is regis-tered with OFSTED*, or approved by your Local Authority (see the list on page 72).

How much will you get?

The grant is based on actual childcare costs of up to £135 a week for one child or up to £200 a week if you have two or more children. Up to these limits you will receive a maximum of 85 per cent of your childcare costs throughout the year. Final-year students qualify for help until the last day of the final term. So if you spend £100 a week on childcare, you will get a grant of £85 a week.

Charitable help for student mothers

Student parents who can't get help with childcare costs from the state may be able to obtain help from the Nuffield Foundation* in the form of a grant from the Elizabeth Nuffield Educational Fund. Set up to help women who study to improve their employment prospects, the fund currently gives grants of between £500 and £3,000 to help with the childcare costs of student mothers. Awards are made in March and October and the deadlines for submitting applications are December and July. Application forms can be downloaded from the Nuffield Foundation* website.

For details of how to apply, ask your LEA for a free fact sheet, *Applying for the Childcare Grant in 2002/03 – what you need to know*. If you are not eligible for the Childcare Grant, you may be able to get help with childcare costs through your college or university Hardship Fund.

Help for unemployed parents

Lone parents who don't have a job or who are working fewer than 16 hours a week can get help with childcare costs if they join the New Deal for Lone Parents while training or looking for work. Provided you use registered childcare (see list on page 72), you'll get up to £100 a week towards the cost of childcare for one child, or £150 a week if you have two or more children in registered childcare. For more information, phone the helpline for the New Deal for Lone Parents★, or go to its website. The National Council for One Parent Families★ can also provide information on benefits available for lone parents.

Employing a nanny

Taking on a nanny also means taking on the duties of being an employer. This means that you become responsible for:

- drawing up a contract of employment
- deducting your nanny's income tax and National Insurance from his or her pay under the Pay As You Earn (PAYE) system

---

Nanny agencies

If you use an agency to find a nanny, the fee can be the equivalent of several weeks' of your nanny's pay. So to make sure that you receive what you hope you are paying for, check that the agency adheres to the Government's voluntary code of practice for nanny agencies. Agencies that do follow the code must carry out relevant background checks and verify qualifications. If you have a complaint about an agency's conduct, contact the Employment Agency Standards Helpline*. This provides a free and confidential complaints service and will investigate any complaints made by families or nannies.

- making the employer's National Insurance contribution
- ensuring that you meet the requirements of the National Minimum Wage.

Drawing up a contract of employment

You are legally obliged to give your nanny a written statement of what the job entails within two months of the nanny starting work. But it's useful for both of you to draw up a written contract of employment before he or she starts work so that it is clear what each of you expect from the other. The contract should give:

- the date your nanny will start work
- the length of employment (your nanny should stay for a minimum of one year)
- details of how much notice he or she must give before stopping working for you
- the hours of work
- the number of days of holiday (which must be no fewer than 20 days including bank holidays)
- the salary (before deducting tax and National Insurance)
- details of what you will pay should the nanny fall ill
- a job description
- details of what you consider to be sackable offences.

For a small fee, you can get a sample contract of employment for nannies from Parents at Work★ (a charity that also publishes free fact sheets on a range of issues affecting working parents), which can be adapted to suit your own circumstances. Alternatively – and again for a small fee – the Professional Association of Nursery Nurses★ provides an information pack, 'All you need to know about working as a Nanny', which contains a sample contract of employment, describes the duties that nannies are normally expected to undertake, and offers advice on current pay scales and insurance issues.

Becoming a tax collector

If you can get away with paying your nanny less than £4,615 a year or £89 a week (in the 2003–4 tax year) – which you may be able to do if he or she works for you part-time (but see 'The National Minimum

Wage' below) – there will be no tax or National Insurance (NI) to deduct from your nanny's pay. However, if – as is more likely – you pay your nanny more than this 'primary threshold', you should contact the Inland Revenue New Employers' Helpline★, which will provide guidance on how to deduct tax and NI, as well as provide help in calculating the tax and NI division for nanny shares. The Inland Revenue should also be able to tell you whether you can use the Simplified PAYE Deduction Scheme, which is the PAYE scheme for people who employ domestic staff whose taxable pay is less than £700 a month.

TIP

If you can't face all the extra paperwork and having to do the calculations yourself, for about £200 a year you can employ a specialist payroll service such as Nannytax* to do it all for you.

The National Minimum Wage

Nannies who live out – or daily nannies – are covered by minimum wage rules. This means that until October 2003 you must pay them at least £3.60 an hour if under 22 or £4.20 an hour if 22 or over. This translates into yearly rates, assuming a 35-hour week, of £6,552 and £7,644. From 1 October 2003 the hourly rates go up to £3.80 and £4.50. From October 2004, the rates may go up to £4.10 and £4.85, subject to a review by the Low Pay Commission. You can find out

---

WARNING

Don't be tempted to pay your nanny less than the minimum wage if he or she is entitled to it – broadly, if he or she is over 18 and lives out, or you provide accommodation that is separate from that of your family. Workers entitled to the minimum wage are also entitled to back payments for periods when they were being paid less than they should have been. So not paying enough could mean that you could face a hefty bill in the future for any shortfall.

---

more about the National Minimum Wage by phoning the National Minimum Wage Helpline*, or by going to the website for Tailored Interactive Guidance on Employment Rights*.

Taking on an au pair

Au pairs are not entitled to the minimum wage because, strictly speaking, they are not employees. An au pair is supposed to live as a member of your family – principally to learn English – and to help out with light domestic work and looking after children.

Au pairs coming to the United Kingdom from within the European Union (EU) do not need a visa, but those from outside the EU do. The special au pair visa is usually given for 12 months (but it can be renewed), and the visa says that an au pair from outside the EU must:

- not work more than five hours a day
- not stay for more than two years as an au pair (but a non-EU national may be able to get a student visa once the two years is up)
- be given free board and lodging, including a room of his or her own
- be paid a reasonable weekly allowance (usually from £50 to £75 a week)
- have two full days off each week.

Advice on employing an au pair from outside the EU is available from the Immigration and Nationality Directorate*.

Chapter 6

Schooling

In theory, primary and secondary education in the state system are free. So parents who have been footing the bill for pre-school child-care (see Chapter 5) – or who can now return to work after looking after children full-time – should be able to breathe a huge sigh of financial relief when a child starts school. However, in practice, although tuition in state schools is free, an increasing number of schools ask parents for voluntary donations – some parents willingly donate as much as £500 a year – and some schools even expect parents to provide basics such as text books.

But even if parents are not asked to contribute to school funds, they still have to foot the bill for travel to and from school, lunches, snacks and drinks, school uniform and sports kit, school trips, swimming and music lessons and the little extras like pencil cases, rulers and school bags, all of which can add up to an average £800 a year for each primary-school pupil and £975 for children at secondary school (see Table 6.1). Over the eleven years that children spend at school, parents can expect to part with nearly £10,000 for each child. And that doesn't include the cost of extra tuition that a growing number of parents pay for in order to improve a child's academic chances. Extra tuition can add from around £600 to £1,000 per subject to the total cost.

Parents who can't fit their jobs round school hours have to budget for after-school childcare, which costs, on average, around £1,300 even for the cheapest option, which is to use an after-school club if it is available. Keeping children amused in the school holidays can add anything from £350 to £3,000 to the bill.

For more information on the cost of out-of-school childcare and the help available to meet the costs, see Chapter 5. For guidance on finding a tutor for your child, contact the Association of Tutors★.

Table 6.1 What a state education costs

Cost of:	Primary school	Secondary school
clothes and shoes	£170	£185
books	£25	£40
school trips	£60	£110
sports kit	£50	£65
clubs	£60	£35
extras	£40	£35
lunch	£285	£395
transport	£110	£110
Total cost	**£800**	**£975**
Source: School Sums Survey by Norwich Union, August 2002.		

Help with the costs of state education

The only help available to *all* parents of state-school pupils is in the form of free school transport. Local Education Authorities (LEAs) are required by law to provide free transport to pupils whose journey between home and school is more than two miles for children up to the age of eight, and three miles for those of eight years and over.

However, free transport does not have to be provided if a child attends a school that is not the nearest suitable school to the child's home. Transport policies vary from one LEA to another, so check with your LEA whether your child qualifies for free transport. The website of the Department for Education and Skills★ also provides information on school transport policies around the country.

Help for low-income families
Most of the other help available with the costs of state schooling is targeted at families on low incomes (see Chapter 4) and comes in the form of:

- **free school meals** for parents who qualify for the maximum amount of Child Tax Credit (see Chapter 4)
- **a uniform allowance** for parents who are claiming Income Support and Income-based Jobseeker's Allowance.

In addition, from September 2004, all 16- to 18-year-olds from low-income families who stay on at school to do a recognised qualification will be able to claim a weekly allowance of up to £30. The amount of the allowance will be determined by a means test of parental income (the exact figures had not been announced at the time of writing) and will be paid only if a pupil keeps to the terms of a 'learning agreement' made with the school or college.

The Education Maintenance Allowance – which aims to encourage more pupils to stay on at school for the sixth form – is available before September 2004 to 16- to18- year-olds who live in one of the areas where the scheme has been piloted. More information is available on the website of the Department for Education and Skills★.

A halfway house

If you don't want – or can't afford – to pay for a private education but you are not happy with the state schools in your area, one option is to move to the catchment area of a state school which *does* meet with your approval. However, this can be a risky strategy unless you can guarantee that your child will get a place at your ideal school before you move – which can be quite difficult, particularly if it is a popular school. It can also be an expensive option, since houses in the catchment area of a sought-after state school tend to command a premium of anything from 20 to 35 per cent. But if you can guarantee a place in your chosen school and you can afford to pay both the higher price of a property and all the costs involved in moving (see Chapter 10), it is likely to be cheaper than paying school fees.

The cost of private education

The costs of putting a child through state schooling pale into insignificance when compared with the cost of educating your child in the independent sector. Rather then paying out £10,000 over 11 years, fee-paying parents can easily spend that much every year, with a total bill that could be as much as £250,000 if a child is educated privately throughout all his or her school years. But even if you use the state system for primary and pay fees only for secondary education, you could still end up parting with a total of at least £75,000. And those figures don't include the extras such as uniform, music lessons, school trips, books, the cost of exams, stationery and medical supplies, which can add an extra 10 per cent to the yearly fee bill.

Table 6.2 shows the least and the most that parents have to pay for school fees for the academic year starting in September 2003. You can get up-to-date information on school fees by contacting the Independent Schools Council information service (ISCis)★. The ISCis website also provides information on the fees charged by a particular school.

Table 6.2 What yearly school fees cost

Day schools	Lowest	Average	Highest
Pre-prep (age 2 to 7)	£2,900	£3,500	£4,200
Preparatory (age 7 to 13)	£4,800	£7,100	£9,300
Boys' senior (age 11 or 13 to 18)	£6,400	£9,600	£12,800
Girls' senior (age 11 or 13 to 18)	£6,400	£8,300	£10,300
Boarding schools			
Preparatory (age 7 to 13)	£9,300	£12,000	£14,800
Boys' senior (age 11 or 13 to 18)	£11,900	£15,700	£19,600
Girls' senior (age 11 or 13 to 18)	£11,500	£15,400	£19,300
Source: Independent Schools Council information service.			

Parents contemplating whether independent education is an affordable option also need to take into account the fact that school fees tend to go up at a rate which has traditionally been much higher than general inflation. In 2003 – as a result of increases in teachers' pay, pension and National Insurance contributions – parents faced fee increases of as much as 10 per cent, which is four times target inflation of 2.5 per cent. However, the average rise in fees in 2003 was 7 per cent. Table 6.3 shows what the average yearly cost of school fees could be in the future, and gives the total cost of seven years of secondary education assuming that fees continue to rise by 7 per cent each year.

Table 6.3 What school fees could cost in the future

Academic year starting in:	Day schools		Boarding schools	
	Boys' senior	Girls' senior	Boys' senior	Girls' senior
2004	£10,200	£8,900	£16,800	£16,500
2005	£11,000	£9,500	£18,000	£17,600
2006	£11,800	£10,200	£19,200	£18,900
2007	£12,600	£10,900	£20,600	£20,200
2008	£13,500	£11,600	£22,000	£21,600
2009	£14,400	£12,400	£23,600	£23,100
2010	£15,400	£13,300	£25,200	£24,700
Total cost	**£88,900**	**£76,800**	**£145,400**	**£142,600**
Average yearly fees inflated at 7.5 per cent and rounded to nearest £100.				

WARNING

If you are considering private education for your child, don't automatically assume that higher fees mean a superior education. High fees may merely mean that you are paying more for swanky surroundings rather than better-quality teaching. To get a feel for which schools offer value for money in terms of the results they achieve, look out for the unique league table published by the *Financial Times**, which ranks private schools in terms of A-Level points per pound spent on fees.

Help with the costs of private education

Although there are several sources of help with the cost of paying school fees, financial assistance is very hard to come by except in certain very specific circumstances – unfortunately, simply being unable to afford the fees is not one of them. ISCis* states that unless parents can afford to pay the full fees themselves, they should not let their children embark on a private education. Any financial help that is obtained should be regarded as a bonus.

The cost of state boarding schools

If you would like to send your children to boarding school – you are going to work abroad, for example, or think that your child could benefit from learning to live away from home in preparation for going off to university – but an independent boarding school is pro-hibitively expensive, the alternative is a state boarding school. Education at state boarding schools – of which there are 35 in the UK – is free, as in all state schools. The charges for boarding range from £3,000 to £6,000 a year.

Run by Local Education Authorities, state boarding schools may take day pupils as well as boarders, and range from mixed-ability and co-educational to selective and single sex. Most are secondary schools, although one or two cater for the very young and several take siblings of primary-school age who will attend the local day school. Two are sixth-form colleges. Admission requirements vary according to the type of school.

For more information about state boarding schools, contact the State Boarding Information Service (STABIS)*, which publishes a free booklet, *Parents' Guide to Maintained Boarding Schools*, avail-able to download from the STABIS website or from the DfES Pupil Wellbeing and Transport Team*. The Boarding Schools Association* provides advice on boarding in both the state and independent sec-tors. Members of HM Forces can obtain details from Service Children's Education (UK)*.

Scholarships and bursaries

Around a third of parents receive help with fees – either in full or in part – in the form of scholarships and bursaries awarded to their talented children.

- **Scholarships** are generally awarded on merit following a competitive test.
- **Bursaries** reduce fees by around 15 per cent or more, and are generally awarded on the basis of academic achievement together with a means test of parental income.

You will find more information on grants and scholarships in the free leaflet, *How You Can Afford an Independent Education*, available from ISCis*.

Foundation awards

Foundation awards are scholarships that are available only to children within a certain category, usually those who live locally. The school's founding document will state the criteria and number of awards that can be made in any one year. Foundation awards are usually based on an assessment of the parents' income and applicants' results following an examination.

Help for the musically and artistically gifted

Some schools offer music scholarships to children who are musically gifted. You can get details of the schools that award music scholarships from the Music Masters and Mistresses Association*. For details of free or heavily subsidised places for choristers at independent choir schools, contact the Choir Schools' Association*. The Government also provides funding for talented pupils of music and dance under the Aided Pupils' Scheme for Music and Dance. Contact the DfES Music and Dance Scheme Team* or go to the website of the Department for Education and Skills*.

Help for particular groups

Some schools offer grants to the children of clergy, teachers and those in the armed forces. Others are prepared to charge reduced fees if parents are former pupils, single parents, or parents sending more than one child to the school. Government grants may be available for the children of members of the Diplomatic Service or the armed forces, or for children with special needs. Note that such financial help may be viewed as a taxable perk, so check with your Tax Office. However, tax on the benefit of having fees paid for you will still cost less than paying the fees yourself.

Charitable help

The number of applications for help from educational charities exceeds the money available, so it would be unwise to rely on getting help from this sort of source. However, educational charities are willing to consider giving financial help with fees, provided that a school is also prepared to help by awarding a scholarship or bursary and:

- you are a single parent with a child over eight years old who faces severe social, emotional or health problems and would benefit from going to a boarding school

- your child has special needs and suffers social and emotional problems as a result
- you have been hit by unexpected financial difficulties and your child is either at a crucial stage in his or her education, or is predicted to achieve A★ and A grades in his or her GCSEs, but, because of the sudden financial difficulties, would not be able to continue at school or stay on into the sixth form.

More information on funding from educational charities is available in the free leaflet, *A Guide to Charitable Funding for Education*, published by ISCis★.

Do-it-yourself independent education

If you cannot afford school fees but you are not happy with your local state schools, an alternative is to educate your child at home. You are entitled to do this provided you can satisfy the education authorities that the education you supply is adequate and suited to the child's age, ability and aptitude. You do not need to hold any specific qualifications or to give formal lessons. You must register with your Local Education Authority, which will allocate you an education officer to provide support and advice. For more information on educating your child at home, contact Education Otherwise*, which provides local help to parents educating their children at home. The Advisory Centre for Education* can also provide advice and information.

Coping with the cost of private education

Parents who manage to plan ahead for the cost of school fees (see page 92) are in the minority. Most parents don't make the decision to send a child to private school until it becomes clear that state schooling is not an acceptable option – a child fails to get a place at a chosen state school, for example – and so don't have the chance to build up savings to pay for school fees. But, staggeringly, given that paying school fees means parting with a minimum of £2,000 three times a year for senior-school education, most parents manage to pay fees out of income.

TIP

Many schools permit and even encourage parents to pay school fees by monthly direct debit. Ask if this option is available, as it will enable you to spread payments throughout the year.

Borrowing to pay fees

For parents whose family budget would be severely stretched by the prospect of paying fees, the alternative is to borrow the money to pay them. If you own your own home, and it is worth more than the amount of your mortgage, one of the most cost-effective ways of borrowing for fees is to switch to a flexible mortgage. Unlike a conventional mortgage, where the amount of the loan is fixed, a flexible mortgage allows you to increase the size of your loan up to a pre-agreed level (which is usually the lower of 75 to 85 per cent of the property's value or three-and-a-half times your before-tax income). You can also make overpayments without having to pay the penalty fees that are charged with many conventional mortgages.

Up-to-date information on the best flexible-mortgage deals is published in the personal finance pages of the weekend press, or go to *www.moneyfacts.co.uk*. If you would like help in finding a good deal, use an independent mortgage broker such as London and Country Mortgages★, Chase de Vere Mortgage Management★ or Charcol Mortgage Brokers★.

Affinity cards

As a way of raising money, some schools operate an affinity card in conjunction with a bank, which offers parents a credit card with an interest-bearing current account and cheque book. You use the card to pay school fees at the beginning of term and then repay what you've borrowed as you would with a credit card. The school receives a donation of, say, £5 for each cardholder and a percentage of the amount spent on the card. However, this sort of scheme is likely to be much more expensive than borrowing using a flexible mortgage.

Planning ahead

If you have time to plan ahead, it is worth doing so even if you do not manage to save the full cost of the fees. Although you can use specially designed school-fee plans, there is no particular reason to do so. There is nothing magical about them, since they are simply a way of investing money in order to make a set of payments sometime in the future.

School-fee plans may take the hassle out of planning for school fees – and introduce an element of discipline to your savings – but there is no reason why you cannot come up with a do-it-yourself plan using other investments. Which you choose will depend on:

- how long there is to go before you need to start paying the fees
- how much risk you are prepared to take with your money
- how flexible you want to be about how you eventually use the money
- whether you can commit yourself to saving on a regular basis
- your tax position
- whether you have a lump sum to invest.

For details of how to work out how much you need to save, see Chapter 10. For more information on suitable savings and investments, see Chapter 12. If you are not confident about making your

---

TIP

One very good reason for avoiding specially packaged school-fee plans is that they are usually based on insurance-based savings plans (also called endowment policies). These require a commitment to save a fixed amount of money for a fixed amount of time – typically ten years. If you fail to keep your savings going for the length of time required, you may find that the money you have carefully put aside for school fees is worth less than you have paid in. You should definitely avoid these plans if you cannot save on a regular basis, or if there is a chance that you will have to stop or reduce your savings – your income falls when you have another child, for example.

---

own investment decisions, it would be a good idea to use the services of an Independent Financial Adviser (IFA), who should be able to work out how much you need to save. SFIA★ specialises in giving independent advice on planning for school fees and has a useful website on which you can work out what fees will cost in the future. To find other IFAs who specialise in school-fee planning, contact the Society of Financial Advisers★. IFA Promotion★ also gives information on finding an adviser.

Paying fees in advance

If you have a lump sum that you can set aside for school fees, as well as investing it you may have the option of pre-paying fees if you have a particular school in mind. The bursar of the school will be able to tell you if the school runs what are often called 'composition fee' schemes. The advantages are that you may be able to buy fees at today's prices; the disadvantage is that if your child does not pass the entrance exam, you may find that you get back less than you handed over unless you can use the money to pay for fees for another child. However, some schools that offer a composition-fee scheme are willing to transfer the pre-paid fees to another school so that you are not irrevocably committed to a particular school. You will find more details about composition fees in the free leaflet, *How You Can Afford an Independent Education*, published by ISCis★.

Chapter 7

University

Whatever your views on private education, you have to admit that there is one big advantage in sending your child to a fee-paying school. By the time your child goes to university, you will be hardened to the idea of parting with substantial amounts of cash three times a year. Parents who choose the state sector may be in for an expensive shock – but the effect on your finances of possibly having to fund tuition fees and make a contribution to a student's living costs may not be as bad as you think.

What university costs

If you believe the estimates published by financial institutions, it costs at least £20,000 for parents to put their child through a typical three-year degree course. Figures published by the National Union of Students★ suggest that parents who want to foot the entire bill face total costs of more like £22,500 for a student on a three-year course outside London and around £25,000 for a student doing the same-length course in the capital.

However, parents are *not* required to foot the entire bill. The most that the Government expects parents to contribute to a student's expenses at university is just under £7,000 in total for a three-year course if a student chooses the most expensive option, which is to live away from home and study in London. Of this, £1,125 (in the 2003–4 academic year) a year is for the tuition fee which parents (rather than students themselves) are expected to pay and which has to be paid up-front at the start of the academic year. Table 7.1 shows the most that any parent is expected to contribute to tuition fees and living costs in the 2003–4 academic year. But whether you will have to pay the maximum depends on a means test of both of your income and that of your student child and also on where a student lives and studies. The means test also decides how big a student loan your child can take out (see page 102).

Parents of independent students – which includes students over 25, married students, and those who have been self-supporting for at least three years before becoming students – are expected to pay nothing towards the cost of university.

Student support in Scotland

Parents of students whose home and place of study are both in Scotland do not have to pay a yearly tuition fee. Instead, Scottish students themselves may have to pay the Graduate Endowment – a one-off payment for the whole course of £2,030 for students starting a course in the 2002–3 academic year. The Graduate Endowment is payable after a Scottish student graduates, and it can be paid by taking out a student loan (see page 102). For parents of Scottish students who study outside Scotland, the system is the same as for other parents. For more information on the Scottish system of student support, contact the Student Awards Agency for Scotland★.

Table 7.1 The most parents have to pay in the 2003–4 academic year

	Studying in London and living:		Studying elsewhere and living:	
	at home	away from home	at home	away from home
Tuition fee	£1,125	£1,125	£1,125	£1,125
Living costs	£790	£1,235	£790	£1,000
Total	**£1,915**	**£2,360**	**£1,915**	**£2,125**
The amount you are required to contribute in a student's final year is slightly lower than the figures given above.				

Assessing parental income

The means test used to assess how much a parent should contribute looks only at the income of natural and adoptive parents. It does not take into account the income of a step-parent or guardian (unless they are also a child's adoptive parents). If parents live apart, the body responsible for assessing income (your Local Education Authority in England and Wales, the Student Awards Agency for Scotland★ and the Student Support Branch of the Department for Employment and Learning★ in Northern Ireland) decides which parent's income it will take into account.

The income used to assess how much parents have to contribute to university costs is what is referred to as 'residual' income, which is your before-tax income minus the following (called 'disregards'):

- the gross amount of pension contributions to an employer's pension scheme (shown on your P60)
- the gross amount of pension contributions to a stakeholder or personal pension (to find the gross amount, divide the amount you pay to your pension provider by 0.78)
- £2,415 if a parent supports a dependent adult who is not his or her spouse
- the cost of domestic help required as a result of a disability.

When assessing a student's own income, the disregards include:

- earnings from casual work, part-time jobs or holiday jobs while a student
- the first £4,000 of money from a scholarship sponsorship or other award
- the first £1,100 of payments from an employer
- any NHS bursary
- income from a trust
- any teacher-training incentive payment from the Government
- most Social Security benefits
- money from student loans and grants
- payments under the SOCRATES (ERASMUS) programme
- the first £900 of income from any other sources.

You will find more detailed information on how a parent's contribution to university costs is calculated in the free booklet, *Financial support for higher education students in 2003–4 – a guide*, which is available by phoning the Department for Education and Skills Information Line★ or by going to the website of the Department for Education and Skills★.

How much parents have to contribute to university costs

Table 7.2 shows what you might be expected to contribute to your children's university costs in the 2003–4 academic year depending on your income. Note that the maximum you have to pay in any academic year is shared between your children if you have two or more students in the family. So if the maximum you have to pay is £995, for example, and you have two children at university, you will be expected to pay them each £497.50 (that is, £995 divided by two). The parental contribution shown in the table will be reduced by £83 for each dependent child still living in the family home. So if you are expected to contribute £2,360 but you have two other children still at school, for example, your parental contribution will be £2,194 (that is, £2,360 minus two lots of £83). For what parents will be expected to contribute in future academic years, see page 102.

Table 7.2 How much parents actually have to pay in the 2003–4 academic year

Residual income	Studying in London and living:		Studying elsewhere and living:	
	at home	away from home	at home	away from home
£10,000	£0	£0	£0	£0
£15,000	£0	£0	£0	£0
£20,000	£0	£0	£0	£0
£25,000	£469	£469	£469	£469
£30,000	£995	£995	£995	£995
£35,000	£1,521	£1,521	£1,521	£1,521
£40,000	£1,915	£2,048	£1,915	£2,048
£45,000	£1,915	£2,360	£1,915	£2,125
£50,000	£1,915	£2,360	£1,915	£2,125
The amount you are required to contribute in a student's final year is slightly lower than the figures given above.				

Reasons for not footing the entire bill for university costs

Even if you are in the enviable position of having sufficient savings to meet the full cost of putting your offspring through university, paying more than you are required to pay (see page 97) and discouraging your child from taking out a student loan (see page 102) to supplement your contribution may not be the best course of action for the following reasons:

- your child may get a job with an employer who offers debt clearance as part of the salary package (this is becoming increasingly common)
- your child may become a teacher in a shortage subject – such as maths and English – and so qualify for government help with loan repayment (see page 106)
- should your child unfortunately die or become permanently disabled, a student loan would be written off.

Another reason for paying only the amount you are required to pay and encouraging your child to take out a student loan is that the interest charged on the loan – currently 1.3 per cent (but due to change to 3.1 per cent in September 2003) – is lower than the interest you can earn on your savings. So it is better to wait until a child graduates before parting with your cash. But even if you do have sufficient funds to be able to clear your offspring's debts on graduation, because the repayment terms for a student loan are so reasonable (see page 103), you might be better off using the cash to:

- pay off any expensive credit-card debts and bank overdrafts your child may have run up (see page 108)
- fund a deposit on a home for your child (see Chapter 9)
- pay into a pension for your child (see Chapter 12)
- make up the gaps in a child's National Insurance record as a result of being at university by paying voluntary National Insurance contributions on his or her behalf (see Chapter 12).

What parents could pay

According to the National Union of Students★, one of the biggest problems with the current system of student support is that the amount the Government thinks students need to live on (which determines the amount parents are required to pay and the size of student loan a student can take out – see page 102) is not enough to meet the full cost of being a student (see Table 7.3). However, this may change in the future as the Government has promised to review the amount of student support it allows, and, at the time of writing, was conducting a study on the true cost of being a student.

Table 7.3 What it costs to be a student

Costs in the 2003–4 academic year	In London		Elsewhere	
	at home	away from home	at home	away from home
Course costs	£425	£425	£425	£425
Rent	£0	£2,885	£0	£2,055
Utility bills	£0	£400	£0	£400
Food	£535	£1,070	£535	£1,070
Laundry	£0	£105	£0	£105
Clothing	£405	£405	£405	£405
Travel	£725	£725	£465	£465
Leisure	£1,380	£1,380	£1,380	£1,380
Total cost	**£3,470**	**£7,395**	**£3,210**	**£6,305**
Maximum help with living costs	**£3,165**	**£4,930**	**£3,165**	**£4,000**
Shortfall	**£305**	**£2,465**	**£45**	**£2,305**

Figures are based on estimated average student expenditure in the 2002–3 academic year inflated by 2.5 per cent to give estimates for the 2003–4 academic year.
Source: National Union of Students.

In the meantime, most students plug the gap between income and outgoings by making full use of the interest-free overdrafts offered to students (see page 108) and around half of students take part-time jobs or work in the holidays to supplement their income. The alternative is for parents to stump up the extra cash. Table 7.4 shows how much you might have to part with to ensure that your student child isn't left short of money.

Table 7.4 How much parents could choose to pay in the 2003–4 academic year

Residual income	Studying in London and living:		Studying elsewhere and living:	
	at home	away from home	at home	away from home
£10,000	£305	£2,465	£45	£2,305
£15,000	£305	£2,465	£45	£2,305
£20,000	£305	£2,465	£45	£2,305
£25,000	£774	£2,934	£514	£2,774
£30,000	£1,300	£3,460	£1,040	£3,300
£35,000	£1,826	£3,986	£1,566	£3,826
£40,000	£2,220	£4,513	£1,960	£4,353
£45,000	£2,220	£4,825	£1,960	£4,430
£50,000	£2,220	£4,825	£1,960	£4,430

Figures include the amount that parents are required to pay towards the tuition fees and living costs (see Table 7.2).

What parents will have to pay in the future

The Government has hinted that it is considering treating students as financially independent of their parents, which would mean that, in the future, there would be no requirement for parents to contribute to a student child's university costs.

Student insurance

When students arrive at university, they are usually offered the chance to buy insurance to cover their belongings at their term-time address. According to insurers who offer student policies, it is usually the parents who end up paying the £100 or so a year that the National Union of Students (NUS)* says it can cost to insure an average student's possessions – typically worth around £3,000. However, buying a separate policy for a student child may be an unnecessary extra expense if:

- parents have taken out – or are prepared to pay extra for – personal possessions cover as an add-on to their own house contents policy
- a parents' policy automatically covers 'items temporarily away from the home' against the standard risks of fire, flood and theft after a break-in

---

The Government has also proposed to abolish the up-front payment of tuition fees from the start of the 2006–7 academic year. If this proposal goes ahead, instead of parents being expected to pay the tuition fee in a lump sum at the start of the academic year, students will be expected to pay the fee – but not until after graduating. The fee will be repaid through the tax system in the same way as student loans are (see page 103). The downside of this proposal is the fact that universities in England (but not in Wales and Scotland) will be able to charge fees of up to a maximum of £3,000 – although the Government will continue to meet the first £1,125 of a student's tuition fee where parental income is £20,000 or less and will make a contribution to tuition fees where parental income is between £20,000 and £30,000. Universities will be permitted to increase fees only if they can prove that they are reaching out to students from all backgrounds. Table 7.5 shows what parents will have to contribute in the future in terms of today's money. For the actual amount you might have to pay in the future, taking inflation into account, see page 112.

For more information on the proposed reforms to parental contributions and student funding, phone the Student Support Information Line★ or go to the website of the Department for Education and Skills★. The proposals are described in detail in the free leaflet, *The future of higher education: what it means to students and*

- insurance is already included in the rent, which is increasingly common for students who live in university halls of residence.

Even if it is necessary to buy insurance for a student's possessions, buying the policy offered on arrival at university may not provide the best deal. The price of insurance varies according to a student's term-time address and the type of accommodation a student lives in. Endsleigh★ is the best-known student insurer, but it is not always the cheapest – especially not for students living in privately rented accommodation – so it's worth getting quotes from less-well-known student insurers such as Campus Insurance★ and Saxon★ (which provides many of the block policies for university halls of residence).

Table 7.5 Maximum yearly parental contribution in the future

Academic year starting in:	Studying in London and living:		Studying elsewhere and living:	
	at home	away from home	at home	away from home
2003	£1,915	£2,360	£1,915	£2,125
2004	£1,915	£2,360	£1,915	£2,125
2005	£1,915	£2,360	£1,915	£2,125
2006	£790	£1,235	£790	£1,000

parents, which is available from the phone line and to download from the website. For more on the grants that will be available to students from low-income households in the future, see page 107.

Other help for students

As well as living off money from parents, students can raise money to meet living costs by applying for a loan from the Government-backed Student Loans Company★, for which all students are eligible (see below). Some students are also eligible for Government help in the form of non-repayable grants (see page 105). Help with living costs as a student is also available from various charitable trusts (see page 107) and from banks (see page 108).

Help for all students

Parents should not feel guilty about letting their student children take out student loans from the Government because these loans are so heavily subsidised – and the Government has rejected calls for interest on student loans to be charged at a commercial rate. Interest on the loan is linked to inflation in September each year so the amount borrowed does not rise in real terms and repayments are reasonable (see page 103). What parents should worry about is the fact that the amount students can borrow is currently insufficient to meet the real cost of being a student (see page 99).

How much students can borrow
All students are eligible to borrow the minimum student loan available, but whether a student can borrow more than this depends on a means test of parental income. Table 7.6 shows the minimum and

maximum loans available to students in higher education in the 2003–4 academic year.

Higher loan amounts are available for students on courses lasting longer than 45 weeks and for students who study abroad for a minimum of eight weeks as part of their course. You will find more detailed information on student loans in the free booklet, *Financial support for higher education students in 2003/2004 – a guide*, available by phoning the Department for Education and Skills Information Line★ or by going to the website of the Department for Education and Skills★.

Table 7.6 Student loans in the 2003–4 academic year

	Studying in London and living:		Studying elsewhere and living:	
	at home	away from home	at home	away from home
Loan available in all years except final year				
minimum	£2,375	£3,695	£2,375	£3,000
maximum	£3,165	£4,930	£3,165	£4,000
Loan available in the final year				
minimum	£2,070	£3,205	£2,070	£2,605
maximum	£2,765	£4,275	£2,765	£3,470

Repaying a student loan

The way in which repayments of a student loan are structured means that they could easily be mistaken for graduate tax. Repaying a student loan differs from the way a loan from a commercial lender is repaid in several important respects:

- a student loan does not have to be repaid until the April after a student graduates (or drops out of a course)
- loan repayments are 'income contingent', which means that repayment of a student loan is linked to a graduate's earnings rather than to the size of the loan
- repayments are collected by the Inland Revenue through the tax system – either though Pay As You Earn (PAYE) for graduates who are employees or through the system of Self Assessment for those who are self-employed
- there is no fixed end date for clearing the debt
- the debt is written off if it hasn't been repaid by the time a graduate dies or reaches 65

- student loans do not appear on a graduate's credit record so, contrary to what some financial institutions claim, they do not affect a graduate's ability to get a mortgage or any other type of loan.

Repayments do not start until a graduate's earnings (or before-tax profits) rise above £10,000. For graduates earning more than £10,000, the monthly repayment is one-twelfth of 9 per cent of gross earnings (minus pension contributions) over £10,000. From April 2005, graduates will not have to start repaying their loans until their earnings rise above £15,000. Graduates who become teachers may qualify to have their loans repaid for them (see page 106). Table 7.7 shows how much the monthly repayments of a student loan will be both before and after April 2005.

Table 7.7 Student-loan repayments

Income [1]	Monthly repayments until April 2005	Monthly repayments after April 2005
£5,000	£0	£0
£10,000	£0	£0
£15,000	£37.50	£0
£20,000	£75	£37.50
£25,000	£112.50	£75
£30,000	£150	£112.50
[1] After deducting pension contributions.		

WARNING

Although some financial institutions – particularly those promoting savings plans – claim that having a student loan to repay is a barrier to graduates who want to get a foot on the property ladder, they are wrong. The main barrier is the high price of houses. Having a student loan to repay does not affect a graduate's ability to get a mortgage. Parents who have the resources to be able to repay a graduate's loan and who want to help out their child financially should consider using the money to fund the deposit on a property instead (see Chapter 9).

Help for some students

In addition to being able to take out a student loan to fund living costs, some students may also be entitled to grants (which do not have to be paid back). Grants that are available include those for:

- students who are parents themselves (see Chapters 4 and 5)
- students in financial difficulties (see below)
- disabled students (see below)
- students who were in care before going to university (see page 106)
- students on teacher-training courses (see page 106)
- students training to be health professionals (see page 107)
- students whose family home is in Wales (see page 107)
- students from low-income households (see page 107).

Help for cases of hardship

Students who find themselves in financial difficulties – which is often the case if a student has only the maximum student loan to live on, or has parents who have refused to pay their contribution to university costs – can apply to their university for a payment from the institution's own Access or Hardship Fund. The alternative is for a student to apply for a Hardship loan of up to £500 from the Student Loans Company⋆. Students studying in Wales can apply for help through the Financial Contingency Funds scheme.

In the future, students in financial difficulties in England will be able to apply for a non-repayable payment from the college's or university's Access to Learning Fund, which replaces all the current forms of help for cases of hardship from the 2004–5 academic year. Students in need of help should approach their student support and welfare service for more details.

Help for disabled students

Disabled students can apply for the Disabled Students' Allowance, which is worth up to £1,490 a year. Disabled postgraduates can claim an allowance of up to £5,370. In addition, disabled students can claim:

- a specialist equipment allowance of up to £4,460 for the whole course
- a non-medical helper's allowance of up to £11,280 a year.

These extra grants for disabled students are not means-tested. For more information on the allowances available to disabled students, get hold of the free guide, *Bridging the Gap*, from the Department for Education and Skills★.

Help for students formerly in care

Students who were in care for at least three months following their sixteenth birthday can apply for the Care Leavers' Grant, which is worth up to £100 a week and is paid only during the summer holidays by the student's assessment body. Students who qualify can get information from their social worker or from the website for care leavers at *www.doh.gov.uk/surviveoutthere/index.htm*.

Help for trainee teachers

Students on one-year, full-time postgraduate teacher-training courses in England leading to qualified teacher status automatically qualify for a Training bursary of £6,000 paid directly to them by the teacher-training college at which they are training. In addition, trainee teachers who are studying to be a teacher in a secondary shortage subject can apply for a means-tested grant of up to £7,500. Shortage subjects include: maths, science, modern languages, design and technology, information and communications technology, geography, music and religious education.

Teacher trainees on undergraduate teacher-training courses in Wales automatically receive a Training grant of £6,000 and can also apply for a Secondary Undergraduate Placement Grant worth £1,000 if they will be teachers of secondary shortage subjects including: maths, science, design and technology, information technology, modern languages, English, drama, and Welsh. £600 is available for students on other undergraduate secondary subject courses.

Students who need help with their Welsh-language skills in order to be able to teach in Welsh – and who intend to look for a job in a Welsh-speaking school – can apply for the Welsh medium incentive supplement, which is worth £1,200.

In whichever country they are studying, teacher trainees who begin teaching a shortage subject in the 2002–3, 2003–4 and 2004–5 academic years are eligible to have their student loans repaid for them by the Government for up to ten years and provided they remain in post at a state school or sixth-form college.

More information on special grants in both England and Wales is available from either the Teaching Information Line★ or the Welsh Language Teaching Information Line★ (for grants in Wales only).

Help for trainee health professionals

Undergraduate medical and dental students living in England or Wales are eligible for NHS bursaries and help with tuition fees from their fifth year of study onwards. More information for students in England is available in the free booklet, *Financial Help for Health Care Students*, available from the NHS Student Grants Unit★. A free booklet, *Financial Help for Health Care Students in Wales*, is available from the NHS (Wales) Student Awards Unit★. Details of NHS bursaries in Northern Ireland are available from The Department of Health (Northern Ireland)★, while medical and dental students in Scotland should contact the Student Awards Agency for Scotland★.

Help for Welsh students

Students whose family home is in Wales can apply for a means-tested Assembly Learning Grant, which is worth up to £1,500 a year. Introduced in the 2002–3 academic year, the grant is aimed at students from low-income families. Information is available from Welsh Local Education Authorities and also at *www.learning.wales.gov.uk* (*www.dysgu.cymru.go.uk* for Welsh speakers).

Help for students from low-income households

From the 2004–5 academic year, students whose family income is below £10,000 will qualify for a government grant of £1,000 to top up income from taking out a student loan and/or money from other grants for which a student may be eligible. Students whose family income is between £10,000 and £20,000 will qualify for a partial grant.

Charitable help for students

Financial help for students is also available from educational trusts and other charities. Lists of trusts which may be prepared to award grants to students are given in the following books, published by the Directory of Social Change★, which should also be available in a local library:

- *A Guide to Local Trusts in Greater London* (£17.95)

- *A Guide to Local Trusts in the South of England* (£17.95)
- *A Guide to Local Trusts in the North of England* (£17.95)
- *A Guide to Local Trusts in the Midlands* (£17.95)
- *A Guide to Scottish Trusts* (£16.95)
- *The Welsh Funding Guide* (£16.95)
- *A Guide to the Major Trusts*, Volumes 1 to 3 (Volumes 1 and 2 cost £20.95 each; Volume 3 costs £17.95).

It is often worth approaching local trusts rather than national trusts, since they receive fewer applications for grants. Other useful publications include:

- **Student Support Sponsorship Funding Directory**★, which lists 2,500 scholarships with information on eligibility and application dates
- **The Grants Register**★, which contains details of over £2,850 awards available to students studying both in the United Kingdom and abroad.

Alternatively, you can search for scholarships, sponsorships, prizes and hardship awards above the value of £250 on the database provided on the website of Scholarship Search UK★.

Help from banks

The vast majority of students sensibly top up the income they get from parents and the student loan by making full use of the interest-free overdrafts on offer from high-street banks. These typically provide interest-free credit of up to £1,000 in the first year of study, rising to up to £2,000 in the final year. Most banks also provide interest-free overdrafts after graduation to ease the transition from student life to real life. Some banks make an interest-free overdraft available to graduates for only one year after leaving university, while others cushion recent graduates from financial reality for up to three years.

Banks also offer credit cards aimed at students. But while these offer student-friendly extras such as cash-back on purchases and discounts at book and record shops, they don't make concessions on interest rates. So, if possible, parents should discourage student children from borrowing on credit cards unless they have the discipline – and resources – to clear their spending in full every month.

Cutting the cost of calls

According to a survey by Virgin Mobile, around 20 per cent of students spend more than £40 a month (£480 a year) on paying for their mobile phones, which can be a big chunk out of a student's already overstretched budget. A lot of students pay more than they need because they wrongly believe that a pay-as-you-go tariff is the best option. However, mobile-phone companies say that – unless a pay-as-you-go phone is genuinely used only for emergencies or in-bound calls – changing to a monthly calling plan works out substantially cheaper largely because of the free texts and inclusive minutes that monthly calling plans provide. Students can also save money on their mobiles by looking out for the special deals available to students from the various networks or mobile-phone dealers such as studentmobiles.com (part of Carphone Warehouse).

Coping with the costs

Parents who have been paying school fees will have no problems meeting the expense of putting their children through university, because university costs are lower than school fees (see Chapter 6). Nor will parents who have at least £7,000 in savings, because this is enough to cover the most they will be required to pay by the Government (see page 95) for a three-year course at the most expensive option of a student living away from home and studying in London. Parents who would prefer to pay their children more than the maximum required by the Government so that their children have enough to live on (see page 100) need savings of around £14,500 to be able to do this.

Paying university costs out of income

Since parents are not expected to pay the total amount of university costs all in one go at the start of a course, it may be possible to meet the costs out of income. Table 7.8 shows the amounts you will have to part with at the start of each term, assuming your child is starting at university in autumn 2003.

Table 7.8 Termly cost of parental contributions for a three-year course

	Studying in London and living:		Studying elsewhere and living:	
	at home	away from home	at home	away from home
2003–4 academic year				
Autumn term	£1,390	£1,540	£1,390	£1,460
Spring term	£265	£410	£265	£335
Summer term	£265	£410	£265	£335
2004–5 academic year				
Autumn term	£1,420	£1,570	£1,420	£1,455
Spring term	£270	£420	£270	£340
Summer term	£270	£420	£270	£340
2005–6 academic year				
Autumn term	£1,455	£1,600	£1,455	£1,525
Spring term	£275	£435	£275	£350
Summer term	£275	£435	£275	£350
Figures assume inflation of 2.5 per cent.				

Borrowing to pay university costs

For parents whose family budget would be severely stretched by the prospect of paying university costs, the alternative is to borrow the money to pay them. If you own your own home, and it is worth more than the amount of your mortgage, one of the most cost-effective ways of borrowing for fees is to switch to a flexible mortgage. Unlike a conventional mortgage, where the amount of the loan is fixed, a flexible mortgage allows you to increase the size of your loan up to a pre-agreed level (which is usually the lower of 75 to 85 per cent of the property's value or three-and-a-half times your before-tax income). You can also make overpayments without having to pay the penalty fees that are charged with many conventional mortgages.

Up-to-date information on the best flexible-mortgage deals is published in the personal finance pages of the weekend press, or go to *www.moneyfacts.co.uk*. If you would like help in finding a good deal, use an independent mortgage broker such as London and Country Mortgages★, Chase de Vere Mortgage Management★ or Charcol Mortgage Brokers★.

Planning ahead

If you do not think that you will be able to meet university costs out of income, but do not want to borrow the money to finance your parental contribution when the time comes, the alternative is to plan ahead.

Using existing savings

If you already have savings and investments, the simplest approach is to earmark a lump sum of around £7,000 for each of your children destined for further education. This is the total cost of a three-year course in today's money. So provided the lump sum grows at a rate equal to or greater than inflation, it should be more than enough to meet the amount you are expected to contribute. But, if you want to play safe, set aside a sum equal to the current cost of a four-year course, which is around £10,000 for the most expensive option.

Which type of investments you choose depends both on how long there is to go until your child starts at university and how much risk you are prepared to take. With fewer than five years in which to save, deposit-based investments such as cash Individual Savings Accounts, savings accounts from banks and building societies and tax-free Savings Certificates from National Savings & Investments are probably most suitable.

If there are more than five years in which to save, equity-based investments are an option, provided you move them into less risky investments a year or so before you need to spend the money. For more on investing money for future spending, see Chapter 10.

Saving up

If you do not have a lump sum you can set aside to fund university costs, you need to start saving on a regular basis. The easiest way to work out how much you need to save is to:

- take the cost of a three- or four-year course by adding together the yearly contribution for each of the years when you expect your children to be at university (see Table 7.9)
- divide this amount by the number of years before your child is set to start at university
- divide again by 12 to get the monthly amount that you need to save.

Your choice of investment is the same as if you have a lump sum to invest (see above).

Under the present system, both fees and living costs are increased each year in line with price inflation as measured by the Retail Prices Index (RPI). Table 7.9 gives an estimate of the most that you are required to contribute in future academic years. If you are not sure where your child will be living or studying, assume the worst, which is that he or she will choose to live away from home and study in London.

Table 7.9 Yearly university costs in the future

Academic year starting in:	Studying in London and living:		Studying elsewhere and living:	
	at home	away from home	at home	away from home
2003	£1,915	£2,360	£1,915	£2,125
2004	£1,420	£2,415	£1,420	£2,175
2005	£2,005	£2,473	£2,005	£2,225
2006	£850	£1,330	£850	£1,075
2007	£870	£1,365	£870	£1,105
2008	£895	£1,400	£895	£1,130
2009	£915	£1,430	£915	£1,160
2010	£940	£1,470	£940	£1,190
2011	£960	£1,505	£960	£1,220
2012	£985	£1,540	£985	£1,250
2013	£1,110	£1,580	£1,110	£1,280
2014	£1,035	£1,620	£1,035	£1,310
2015	£1,060	£1,660	£1,060	£1,345
2016	£1,090	£1,700	£1,090	£1,375
2017	£1,115	£1,745	£1,115	£1,410
2018	£1,145	£1,790	£1,145	£1,445
2019	£1,170	£1,835	£1,170	£1,485
2020	£1,200	£1,880	£1,200	£1,520
2021	£1,230	£1,925	£1,230	£1,560
2022	£1,260	£1,975	£1,260	£1,600
Figures assume inflation of 2.5 per cent.				

Chapter 8

The gap year

The bad news for parents whose offspring intend to take a gap year – as around 60 per cent of pre-university students do – is that the average gap year costs in the region of £3,000, although the cost can be as much as £6,000. The good news is that, according to gapyear.com* – a specialist gap-year information website – the majority of 'gappers' raise most, if not all, of the money they need through a combination of work and sponsorship. But even if you do have the resources to be able to fund a gap year in full, research suggests that you will be doing your children a favour if you *don't* foot the entire bill. Universities and employers – the majority of which take a positive view of gap years – are far more impressed by young people who have funded and organised their gap year themselves. Even better news for some parents is that around a quarter of pre-university students who take a gap year do so to earn money to meet their university costs.

How parents can help

Although parents may not be required to foot the bill for a gap year, it is likely that they will still be expected to provide some kind of support of both a financial and practical nature including:

- helping to research gap-year options (see page 114)
- checking that a gap-year provider is reputable (see page 115)
- helping to find sources of funding (see page 115)
- buying adequate insurance (see page 116)
- taking precautionary measures for dealing with disaster (see page 119)
- providing money in an emergency (see page 119).

Gap-year options

According to the advice given in the parents' section of gapyear.com⋆, parents should recognise that it is up to the child to decide what to do in his or her gap year. The specialist gap-year website also warns parents not to use money as a bribe in an attempt to influence how a child spends his or her time between school and university. However, it can be helpful for parents to ensure that their pre-university children start planning at least a year in advance and that they look at all the options available to them. These include:

- doing their own thing (aka dossing)
- travelling around the world
- working in the UK or abroad
- doing volunteer work
- joining a structured work experience opportunity
- living abroad on a cultural exchange
- participating in an expedition
- learning a new skill on a course in the UK or overseas.

You will find more detailed information on the opportunities available under each of the options at *www.gapyear.com* and also at *www.gap-year.com*, the website related to *The Gap-Year Guidebook* (£11.95), a publication which is updated annually and contains a wealth of practical information. For opportunities for volunteer work in the UK, contact Community Service Volunteers⋆ or the

---

Help for young volunteers on a low income

Under the Young Volunteer Challenge scheme launched in May 2003, young people from households on incomes of £13,000 or less can qualify for a weekly allowance of £45 if they commit to at least 30 hours' volunteer work a week in the year after they have finished school, college or training. The scheme will largely benefit 18- and 19-year-olds who, if they qualify for the weekly allowance, will also get a lump sum of £750 after successfully completing nine months of volunteering. More information is available from the Department for Education and Skills⋆.

---

charity Worldwide Volunteering★ for volunteering abroad. Details of paid jobs abroad are available at *www.payaway.co.uk*. The website *www.gap-year.com* has details of jobs both at home and abroad.

Choosing a gap-year company

As the number of gappers has risen over the past few years, so has the number of organisations – including both charities and private companies – which sell year-out programmes. Given the high price of some of these gap-year packages, it is vital that you choose a reputable company and that the organisations are carefully researched before committing any money. If travel to far-flung places is involved, it is also important to address safety issues and ask about the kind of support that is available in emergencies.

You will have a better chance of finding a reputable organisation if you make sure that it belongs to the Year Out Group★, which is a not-for-profit association of leading year-out organisations that is supported by both the Department for Education and Skills★ and the Universities & Colleges Admissions Service (UCAS)★. The aim of the Year Out Group is to:

- promote the concept and benefits of a well-structured year out to both young people and their parents
- provide accurate and impartial information about structured year-out programmes
- help young people and their parents to choose suitable and worthwhile projects
- promote good practice in the gap-year industry through a code of practice which its members are expected to follow.

As part of its commitment to helping parents and their children to find a suitable project, the website of the Year Out Group★ provides a detailed list of questions that should be asked when assessing the suitability of a year-out programme. There is also helpful advice on *gapyear.com*★on checking out gap-year placements.

Funding a gap year

The majority of gappers fund their trips by getting a job. The website *www.gap-year.com* provides contacts for work both in the UK and abroad and gives a list of employers offering seasonal work and those who have specific gap-year employment policies.

An alternative to earning money is to ask for it by applying for grants from both local and national charitable trusts. Local trusts are worth approaching first since they tend to have fewer applications for grants than national charitable trusts. Lists of trusts who are prepared to part with money for worthwhile-sounding gap-year activities (among other things) are given in the following books, published by the Directory of Social Change*, which should also be available in a local library:

- *A Guide to Local Trusts in Greater London* (£17.95)
- *A Guide to Local Trusts in the South of England* (£17.95)
- *A Guide to Local Trusts in the North of England* (£17.95)
- *A Guide to Local Trusts in the Midlands* (£17.95)
- *A Guide to Scottish Trusts* (£16.95)
- *The Welsh Funding Guide* (£16.95)
- *A Guide to the Major Trusts*, Volumes 1 to 3 (Volumes 1 and 2 cost £20.95 each; Volume 3 costs £17.95).

The gapyear.com* website provides guidance on presenting a professional grant application, together with advice on other ways of raising funds to finance a gap year. Members of the Year Out Group* are also able to provide advice on fundraising to meet the cost of their programmes.

CASE STUDY: Ann

When she took a year out from her modern languages course to improve her Italian by studying at a language school in Florence, Ann's living costs were met by a contribution from her parents combined with money from the state. Her language-school fees were met by a grant from a trust that had advertised for applications in the local press.

Gap-year insurance

The likelihood that children who are imminently off on their gap-year travels have thought about insurance is slim. According to the companies that sell gap-year travel insurance, the bulk of such policies are bought by worried parents rather than by the intrepid travellers themselves. In the experience of one travel-insurance specialist, a lack of such insurance may come to light only days before departure and it has even been known for parents of unprepared backpackers to buy policies on Christmas Day.

But even if your son or daughter has thought about buying this essential cover, research by gapyear.com★ suggests that they will spend more time choosing clothes, penknives and other travel accessories than they will finding insurance best suited to their travel plans and budget.

Cover essentials
Guidance issued by the Travel Advice Unit★ of the Foreign & Commonwealth Office (FCO) says that, at a bare minimum, a policy should provide cover for the following.

- **The full length of the trip** The Travel Advice Unit★ stresses that gap-year travellers should not rely on cover under a multi-trip annual travel policy, because these typically limit cover to trips of between 30 and 90 days and so are not suitable for extended periods of travel.
- **All the countries the gapper is planning to visit** This is especially important if travel plans include visits to exotic or unusual places – but bear in mind that most insurers will not provide cover for areas that the FCO has warned against travelling in.
- **Medical emergencies and repatriation** Even if there is a reciprocal health agreement (such as the E111 agreement that applies in Europe) between the UK and the country the gapper is visiting, personal medical cover is still essential, for instance, to cover the cost of returning home (repatriation) following a medical emergency, by air ambulance if necessary. Look for at least £1 million of medical cover in Europe and £2 million in the rest of the world.
- **Personal liability** If the gapper accidentally injures someone or damages their property, this cover pays out for legal expenses (and any damages) if they sue. Look for cover of at least £1 million.

You should also look for policies that provide a 24-hour emergency number and which belong to the Financial Ombudsman Service.

Added extras

It would be unlikely to find that a gap-year policy did not offer these bare essentials. However, policies vary widely in the other cover they offer. Parents of children intending to take advantage of opportunities to try a bunjee jump, go scuba diving, white-water rafting or any other equally risky pursuit should pay particular attention to cover for hazardous activities. With some policies, only those activities specified at the time the policy is taken out are covered and then only if an additional premium is paid. Since you may not know what your children are going to get up to, you would be better off with a policy that automatically includes cover for hazardous activities.

Insurers also differ in their attitude to skiing. Some include medical cover for injuries as a result of indulging in winter sports as standard, while others charge extra to arrange cover for skiing.

Travellers who plan to supplement their travel costs by working their way round the world should also make sure that their policy covers them for work-related accidents. Young people who will be studying abroad as well as travelling should also check that a policy provides appropriate cover.

As with normal travel insurance, baggage and personal belongings are covered under a gap-year policy, but if your children won't be taking anything worth stealing, they could consider a budget policy that doesn't provide cover for belongings.

What gap-year insurance costs

Table 8.1 shows the typical cost of gap-year policies according to the length of time a gapper will be away and the part of the world they will be visiting. Cheaper policies are available by buying over the Internet. The following companies offer reasonable deals on gap-year insurance: Boots★, Club Direct★, CostOut.co.uk★ (online only), Direct Line★, Flexicover Direct★, gapyear.com★, Go Travel Insurance★, JourneyWise★, Leading Edge★, Options★ and the Travel Insurance Club★.

Preparing for the worst

Although disaster probably won't strike, it's as well to be prepared and advice on the parents' section of gapyear.com suggests that parents should consider getting their children to draw up a power of attorney, giving parents the power to deal with their affairs while

Table 8.1 What gap-year insurance costs

	Standard policies	Budget policies
6 months		
Europe	£75	£60
Australia and New Zealand	£100	£80
Worldwide excluding USA	£120	£100
Worldwide including USA	£150	£125
12 months		
Europe	£150	£125
Australia and New Zealand	£200	£175
Worldwide excluding USA	£220	£200
Worldwide including USA	£250	£225

they are away. For a modest fee, you can get a solicitor to do this – for details of local solicitors, contact LawNet⋆ – or a Citizens Advice Bureau⋆ can help with drafting the document. Banks usually require customers to fill in a 'third party mandate' if someone wants to permit another person to run their account.

Even if you do not go to the lengths of drawing up a power of attorney, it is definitely worth your child having at least two copies of all documents – one to pack and one to leave behind – and keeping a note of all the emergency phone numbers for reporting credit and debit cards lost or stolen.

Emergency cash

Although most parents do not finance the gap year itself, they are generally called upon to provide emergency funds, either to cover a budgeting blip or to replace money that has been lost or stolen.

The fastest way to send money abroad is by using the money transfer systems offered by Western Union⋆ and MoneyGram⋆, by which money can be transferred within 15 minutes. These services are useful if someone abroad needs foreign cash very quickly, but they can cost from £12 to £45 depending on how much money is being sent and where it is being sent to.

If the need for cash is less urgent and the person abroad could wait three days for the money, the easiest solution – assuming the person in foreign parts has access to cash machines – is to pay money into his or her account in the UK. If parent and child both have accounts at the same bank, it may be possible to make a same-day transfer, so check with your bank.

If the child in need of money does not have access to cash machines, but they are able to wait a few days for the money, parents can ask their bank to transfer money to a nominated bank abroad on a pay-on-identification basis. This enables a cash-strapped gapper to pick up cash at a foreign bank on production of his or her passport. Transferring money in this way can take between one and three days and can cost from £20 to £50 depending on the amount being sent.

Chapter 9

A home of their own

Helping children to get a foot on the property ladder – and so helping them to take advantage of the fact that it is typically cheaper to buy than to rent – is one of the best uses for any spare cash that a parent may have. And it is arguably a much better use for a nest egg than paying off a graduate's student loan (see Chapter 7). However, because of the costs involved in buying a home, it makes sense to help with purchasing a property only once an adult offspring intends to stay in the same place for at least three years, although five years would be preferable.

Barriers to property purchase

Often, the main barrier to buying a property faced by first-time buyers is the large gap between the purchase price of a property and the amount that mortgage lenders are prepared to let them borrow.

How much can they borrow?

The size of loan that a borrower can take out is linked to both the lender's valuation of a property and a borrower's annual income. For someone buying a home on his or her own, the amount a lender is prepared to lend is typically three to three-and-a-half times annual salary, although some lenders are prepared to lend up to four times salary.

A limited number of lenders – including Manchester Building Society, NatWest Mortgage Services and the Royal Bank of Scotland – are prepared to lend up to five times salary. However, these lenders offer to lend on this basis only to people in certain professions and they are unlikely to lend the full price of a property.

Rather than using income multiples, some lenders – including Abbey National, Direct Line, Halifax, Nationwide Building Society, Norwich & Peterborough Building Society, Standard Life Bank and Yorkshire Building Society – link the amount they will lend to a borrower's ability to afford the monthly mortgage repayments.

---

100 per cent mortgages

As a general rule, taking out a mortgage for the full cost of the property should be regarded as a last resort. There are three main reasons for this: if house prices fall, you risk owing more on your mortgage than the property is worth; the interest rate on the mort-gage is likely to be higher than it would be if you put down a deposit; and taking out a 100 per cent mortgage typically means that you have to pay a high lending fee – also called a mortgage indemnity guarantee. This is a one-off lump-sum fee of several hundred pounds (usually added to the loan) paid to buy an insur-ance policy that protects the lender – rather than the borrower – from the risk of not being able to recover the full amount of the loan if the borrower fails to keep up repayments and the property has to be repossessed. The fee is typically 7.5 to 8 per cent of the difference between the amount borrowed and 75 per cent of the valuation.

Other costs involved in buying a home

Although there are a few lenders prepared to advance a mortgage loan equal to the amount of the valuation of a property (see box above), most will lend a maximum of 90 to 95 per cent of the mort-gage valuation (which may be less than the purchase price of the property). First-time buyers therefore need to fund a deposit of at least 5 per cent of the value of the property. However, a deposit of at least 10 per cent is preferable, while 25 per cent is optimal. Table 9.1 shows the average deposit required according to regional house prices.

In addition to finding the money to be able to put down a deposit, first-time buyers will also need sufficient cash to pay the costs involved in buying a home. For further details, see Table 9.2.

Table 9.1 Average deposits for house purchase

Region	5 per cent	10 per cent	25 per cent
East Anglia	£5,260	£10,520	£26,300
East Midlands	£4,300	£8,600	£21,500
London	£9,725	£19,450	£48,625
North	£3,475	£6,950	£17,375
Northern Ireland	£4,370	£8,740	£21,850
North-West	£4,105	£8,210	£20,525
Scotland	£3,825	£7,650	£19,125
South-East	£8,005	£16,010	£24,015
South-West	£5,975	£11,950	£29,875
Wales	£3,945	£7,890	£19,725
West Midlands	£4,840	£9,680	£24,200
Yorkshire & Humberside	£3,685	£7,370	£18,425
Source: Abbey National, January 2003.			

Table 9.2 The cost of buying a home in England and Wales

Property price	Solicitor	Land Registry fees	Searches	Stamp Duty	Total
£50,000	£468	£40	£170	£0	**£678**
£60,000	£475	£60	£170	£0	**£705**
£80,000	£497	£60	£170	£800	**£1,527**
£100,000	£522	£100	£170	£1,000	**£1,792**
£150,000	£576	£150	£170	£1,500	**£2,396**
£200,000	£637	£150	£170	£2,000	**£2,957**
Source: Woolwich plc, *Cost of Moving Survey*, 2003.					

Stamp duty

There is no stamp duty to pay on properties costing up to £150,000 in certain 'designated disadvantaged' areas. A list of almost 2,000 such areas is available on the Stamp Office website at *www.inlandrevenue.gov.uk/so*, where you can search by postcode. If a property is not located in a designated disadvantaged area and its purchase price is over £60,000, you pay stamp duty at a rate of: 1 per cent on properties costing between £60,001 and £250,000; 3 per cent on those costing between £250,001 and £500,000; and 4 per cent on those costing more than £500,000. Stamp duty is payable on the whole price of properties that cost more than £60,000.

How parents can help

Parents who have built up a nest egg for their adult children can make property purchase an affordable option for their offspring by:

- paying off expensive debts such as overdrafts, credit-card debts and personal loans (see below)
- funding the upfront costs of buying property (see page 125).

However, parents who do not have the resources to meet the upfront costs of buying property may still be able to help their children to get a foot on the property ladder by:

- acting as a guarantor on a child's mortgage
- buying a property jointly with a child
- raising the cash for upfront costs by increasing the mortgage on their own property.

Paying off expensive debts

When assessing a mortgage application, lenders look at several factors, including the value of the property, a potential borrower's salary, a person's credit record and the affordability of the mortgage – that is, whether a borrower will have sufficient after-tax income after meeting other outgoings to cover the monthly mortgage repayment.

While a government-backed student loan does not appear on a person's credit record, other loans – such as overdrafts, personal loans and outstanding credit-card debts – do. Lenders also take into account the amount of loan repayments when assessing the affordability of a mortgage. Reducing monthly outgoings by paying off outstanding commercial debts (preferably before a mortgage application is made) can therefore help to make it more affordable to take on what may need to be a substantial mortgage.

Funding the upfront costs of buying property

Giving or lending the money for a deposit and/or the other costs involved in buying property doesn't just help to make a property more affordable by reducing the size of the mortgage and other outgoings, it can also help a first-time buyer to:

- **get a competitive mortgage deal**, because the more a borrower puts towards the cost of a property, the lower the interest rate on the mortgage
- **avoid a high lending fee**, which many lenders charge if a mortgage loan is more than 90 to 95 per cent of the property's valuation for mortgage purposes.

TIP

Several banks and building societies offer regular-savings accounts aimed specifically at people wanting to save for a deposit on a property. The attraction of saving up in one of these home-buyer savings accounts is that they offer the discipline of saving a minimum of £100 a month and the interest rates tend to be higher than on other savings accounts. Another attraction is that they offer cash bonuses if the regular saver eventually becomes a mortgage borrower with the same institution. Some accounts actively encourage parents to pay in money on top of regular savings by the account holder.

Acting as guarantor

Helping out with the deposit on a property is one way of helping your child to secure a mortgage loan. Another – which does not require you to part with a lump sum – is to act as guarantor to an adult child's mortgage. This means that you agree to pay the mortgage if your child cannot. This helps because lenders may be willing to advance a larger loan than they would have done without a parental guarantee.

Lenders who market special graduate mortgages of up to 100 per cent of a property's valuation, all of which require a parental guarantee, include Bank of Scotland Mortgages, Dudley Building Society, Lloyds TSB Scotland and Scottish Widows Bank. Other lenders may be prepared to apply more generous lending limits in exchange for a parental guarantee if you ask them.

CASE STUDY: Ryan and David

Ryan sold some shares to raise the cash both to pay off his son David's post-university credit-card debts and to be able to put down a 10 per cent deposit on a two-bedroomed flat for him. But David, who had been living at his parents' home since leaving university, was able to get a sufficiently large mortgage only by Ryan agreeing to act as guarantor. The mortgage was from a small local building society, which had been featured as a best buy in the personal finance pages of a Sunday newspaper. And although it wasn't advertised as a 'guarantor mortgage', the lender was perfectly happy to take Ryan's guarantee as security against David defaulting on the loan.

Buying a property jointly

The alternative to acting as guarantor is to buy a share in your child's property and take out a mortgage jointly with him or her. This has the advantage that the mortgage will be based on the incomes of both borrowers – and so the amount you can borrow will be larger than if only one person applied for a mortgage – and also means that, as co-owner, you share in any increase in the value of the home. The disadvantage is that if you eventually allow your child to buy out your share, there may be a capital gains tax bill on any gain you make. In addition, this option will be available only if the lender is satisfied that a parent can meet the repayments on both his or her own mortgage as well as those on the joint mortgage with a child.

Increasing your own mortgage

The alternative to buying a property jointly with a child – and also an alternative for parents who do not have savings that they are willing to tie up in property – is to raise cash for a deposit by borrowing against equity in the family home by increasing the parents' own mortgage. However, this is an option only if the value of the parental home is greater than the outstanding mortgage on it. The lender may also refuse to increase the mortgage if the increased repayments do not appear to be affordable.

A halfway house

An option for people who cannot afford to buy a property outright is to buy jointly with a housing association through a shared-ownership scheme which provides a halfway house between renting and buying. Shared ownership means that to start with you buy only part of a home and pay rent on the rest, with the option of buying a bigger share as and when you can afford it. Most shared-ownership schemes are for homes in new or renovated developments run by housing associations and housing trusts. More information on shared-ownership schemes is available from the Shared Ownership Advice Line and from the Housing Corporation*. Information on schemes in Northern Ireland can be obtained from the Northern Ireland Co-ownership Housing Association*, while the Scottish Federation of Housing Associations* can provide details of schemes in Scotland. For shared-ownership schemes in Wales, contact the housing division of the Welsh Assembly*.

Chapter 10

Coping with the costs

It isn't just the additional costs involved in bringing up children that take their toll on the family finances, it is also the inevitable drop in income faced by mothers who make full use of their rights to take time off work when a child is born or adopted (see Chapter 4). Then there are the additional costs that parents face if they need to move to a bigger home to accommodate an increase in the family's size (see page 131) – not to mention the money needed to finance future costs for things like childcare (see Chapter 5), schooling (see Chapter 6) and university (see Chapter 7). Mothers who intend to take an extended career break to bring up young children themselves also need to address the issue of how they will ensure that their future pension doesn't suffer while they are not earning.

Facing up to a fall in income

How drastic a cut in income mothers who intend to make full use of their rights to time off work (see Chapter 4) face depends largely on the generosity of an employer's maternity package. Mothers who are lucky enough to work for an employer who offers full pay for the first six months of maternity leave will cope much better than someone whose employer pays only the legal minimum. Table 10.1 shows what your average monthly income (after tax and National Insurance) would be if your employer pays only what is required by law.

You face the most drastic cut in income if you qualify only for Maternity Allowance of £100 a week (because you are self-employed, for example, or haven't worked for your current employer for long enough to qualify for Statutory Maternity or Adoption Pay), because you do not get the benefit of being paid 90 per cent of earnings for the first six weeks of maternity leave.

Table 10.1 The effect that taking maternity leave has on income

Yearly before-tax earnings before taking maternity leave	Average monthly income for the whole year [1] if you qualify for Statutory Maternity Pay and you go on maternity leave for:		Average monthly income for the whole year [1] if you qualify for Maternity Allowance and you go on maternity leave for:	
	6 months [2]	12 months	6 months [2]	12 months
£10,000	£595	£255	£625	£215
£15,000	£765	£295	£780	£215
£20,000	£930	£340	£920	£215
£25,000	£1,100	£385	£1,060	£215
£30,000	£1,270	£420	£1,200	£215
£35,000	£1,440	£450	£1,340	£215
£40,000	£1,605	£485	£1,480	£215
£45,000	£1,775	£520	£1,620	£215
£50,000	£1,955	£550	£1,760	£215
£55,000	£2,145	£575	£1,900	£215
£60,000	£2,295	£605	£2,040	£215
£65,000	£2,445	£635	£2,190	£215
£70,000	£2,590	£665	£2,350	£215
£75,000	£2,740	£695	£2,475	£215

Figures are for the 2003–4 tax year.
[1] After tax and National Insurance.
[2] Figures assume that you return to full-time work at your pre-maternity-leave salary.

Extra income

On the plus side, as soon as your baby is born – or an adopted child comes to live with you – you will see a modest increase in your monthly income because the state will pay you Child Benefit of £64.20 a month for a first baby and £43 a month for a new sibling (in the 2003–4 tax year). For more on claiming Child Benefit, see Chapter 4.

CASE STUDY: Charlotte and Justin

Apart from the shock of spending more than half of her after-tax salary on childcare for her six-month-old son Justin, Charlotte has seen very little change in her finances. While on maternity leave, her income didn't fall at all because her employer offers a very generous maternity package and pays full pay to mothers on maternity leave, and Charlotte chose to go back to work after only 20 weeks at home. Apart from the childcare bill, the extra expense of having Justin has been negligible. Charlotte 'barely had to buy a thing' when he was born because her twin sister lent her 'masses of clothes' and other baby kit, while generous grandparents bought the car seat and buggy. Charlotte noticed that the nappies and milk swelled the weekly supermarket bill, but says that this increased cost was pretty much cancelled out by the fact that she spends less on going out than she did before.

In addition, the birth of a child combined with the reduction in your income as a result of going on maternity – or adoption – leave may mean that you become eligible for a higher rate of Child Tax Credit, which – if your household income is less than £50,000 – is worth at least £90 a month if you have a new baby and at least £45 a month if the new addition to your family is over one year old. Alternatively, if you weren't eligible for the Child Tax Credit before the birth (or adoption of) a child, your new financial circumstances may mean that you become entitled to it. Broadly, you will be eligible for at least

---

TIP

If your time off work will result in a lower income it is worth checking whether your entitlement to tax credits has changed, which you can do by phoning the New Tax Credits Information Line* or by using the interactive calculator on the Inland Revenue* website. For more on how tax credits are calculated, see Chapter 4. Even if you are not entitled to tax credits, a fall in income may mean that you should get a tax rebate, so contact your Tax Office to see if this applies to you.

---

some Child Tax Credit if your household income is less than £66,000 a year if you have a child under one, or less than £58,000 a year if your child is over one.

Extra expenses

How much having a child will add to your monthly budget will depend entirely on your personal preferences – if you choose to indulge in the latest designer babywear, for example, you will clearly spend more than someone who is happy to make do with cast-off baby kit and hand-me-down clothes. However, as a rough guide, you should budget for at least £150 a month to cover consumables such as food, nappies and clothes, and a further £50 or so for essentials such as life insurance (see Chapter 2).

Mothers who intend to return to work after six months – when paid maternity leave stops – and who do not have access to free childcare, can expect their average monthly outgoings in the first year of a child's life to go up by around £250 a month (that is, the cost of six months' full-time care in a day nursery averaged over the whole year), although the average monthly cost in a child's second year will rise to around £500. For more on childcare costs, see Chapter 5.

The extra expense of moving home

Parents who plan to move house to make space for a new arrival also need to consider the extra costs of moving up the property ladder. Table 10.2 (overleaf) shows the upfront costs involved in moving home and also the extra monthly costs of taking on a bigger mortgage.

CASE STUDY: Jennie

As a self-employed financial consultant, Jennie qualified only for Maternity Allowance of £100 for the first six months of her maternity leave, which meant a potentially drastic cut in her income. However, because she was determined to take an extended career break so that she didn't miss out on her daughter's early years, as soon as she knew she was pregnant, she saved everything she earned. Adjustments to the family budget have meant that Jennie and husband, Nick, are able to survive on Nick's salary alone.

Table 10.2 The cost of moving home

Upgrading from a home worth	Upfront expenses involved in buying and selling	Additional monthly cost of the mortgage [1]
£60,000 to £80,000	£3,005	£110
£80,000 to £100,000	£3,465	£110
£100,000 to £150,000	£4,300	£280
£150,000 to £200,000	£5,525	£280
£200,000 to £300,000	£13,430	£555
£300,000 to £500,000	£20,975	£1,110

[1] Based on a repayment mortgage repaid over 25 years with an interest rate of 4.5 per cent.
Source: Woolwich plc, *Cost of Moving Survey*, 2003.

Budgeting for the costs of having a child

If you want to start a family – or have another child – but you are not sure whether it is a viable option, you may find it helpful to work out how your finances overall will be affected by parenthood and where you need to make adjustments to the amount you spend on other things. Doing this calculation can also help you decide whether you can afford to take unpaid maternity leave or whether you can afford only to take six months' paid leave. To work out how much you need to save – or need to cut down on expenditure:

- **Add up** all the monthly income you would expect to receive for the year in which you will be on maternity leave, including your expected average monthly after-tax income (see Table 10.1 if you want to assume the worst), Child Benefit and any tax credits you might be entitled to (see page 129).
- **Subtract** this figure from your current monthly after-tax salary. This gives you the figure for the average amount of income you will lose by taking time off work to have a baby (or adopt a child).
- **Add** to this figure the amount of additional monthly expenses you will incur, such as the extra monthly costs of having a child, life-insurance premiums, average childcare costs if you plan to return to work after six months and the extra costs of increasing your mortgage if you plan to move.

- **Subtract** the amount of monthly expenditure that would fall – travel expenses, for example, or the cost of socialising. Also subtract expenditure that you would be prepared to do without.

This tells you how much income you need to find a way of replacing if you are to maintain your current standard of living. This could be achieved by saving up before you start a family, for example. It also tells you the amount by which you need to reduce your expenditure – by paying off loans, for example, or by doing without holidays or a gym membership – if saving up is not an option.

TIP

If you have a computer and spreadsheet software, you will save time if you enter the figures on a spreadsheet. This will also help if you need to adjust the figures or if you want to do 'what if' calculations to see the effect of making changes to your spending.

Saving up

Once you have estimated the costs and the likely effect on your income, you can work out how much you need to save – although

---

WARNING

Saving while running expensive debts such as a bank overdraft, personal loan or outstanding balance on a credit card, makes no sense at all because the interest you can earn on your savings is likely to be a lot lower than the interest being paid on debts. If you do have spare cash that you are able to save – or you can *create* spare cash by saving money, by switching your mortgage to a cheaper lender, for example – your priority should be paying off debt. For more on practical ways in which you can create spare cash by saving money on your finances, you may wish to consult *The Which? Guide to Money*, published by Which? Books*.

---

as a rough guide, you should aim to save about six months' worth of after-tax income to tide you over in the first year of having a child. Fathers who intend to take paternity leave should try to save enough money to be able to take both paid and unpaid leave on the birth (or adoption) of a child.

TIP

If you are part of a two-income household and are not sure that you would want to return to work after your child has arrived – or you want to see if giving up work would be a viable option – consider trying to live on the income of the person who would carry on working and saving the other income.

Table 10.3 How long you will have to save for

Lump sum	How long it will take if you can save		
	£50 a month	£100 a month	£250 a month
£5,000	7 years 10 months	4 years	1 year 8 months
£6,000	9 years	4 years 9 months	2 years
£7,000	10 years 3 months	5 years 6 months	2 years 4 months
£8,000	11 years 7 months	6 years 3 months	2 years 8 months
£9,000	12 years 10 months	6 years 11 months	2 years 11 months
£10,000	14 years	7 years 7 months	3 years 3 months
£11,000	15 years 2 months	8 years 4 months	3 years 7 months
£12,000	16 years 3 months	9 years	3 years 10 months
£13,000	17 years 4 years	9 years 8 months	4 years 2 months
£14,000	18 years 5 years	10 years 3 months	4 years 6 months
£15,000	19 years 6 years	10 years 11 months	4 years 9 months
£16,000	20 years 6 years	11 years 7 months	5 years 1 month
£17,000	21 years 6 months	12 years 2 months	5 years 4 months
£18,000	22 years 5 months	12 years 10 months	5 years 8 months
£19,000	23 years 5 months	13 years 5 months	5 years 11 months
£20,000	24 years 4 months	14 years	6 years 3 months
Figures assume an after-tax return on savings of 2.5 per cent.			

How much to save

In an ideal world, prospective parents would start saving towards the costs of having children at least five years before they intend to start a family. In the real world, however, it is unlikely that most people will have the luxury of this much time. It is also highly unlikely that parents will manage to save enough to be able to meet the full cost of bringing up a child. But that doesn't mean that parents should not try to save as much as possible.

Table 10.3 shows how long it would take to amass various levels of savings if you can afford to save only a fixed amount each month. If you are determined to save a particular size of lump sum to meet future costs, see Table 10.4, which tells you how much you need to save each month according to the size of lump sum you are aiming for and the number of years there are to go before you will need to spend the money.

Table 10.4 How much you need to save each month

Lump sum required	How much you need to save if you will need the lump sum in		
	1 year	5 years	10 years
£5,000	£415	£80	£40
£6,000	£495	£95	£45
£7,000	£580	£110	£50
£8,000	£660	£125	£60
£9,000	£745	£140	£70
£10,000	£825	£155	£75
£11,000	£910	£175	£80
£12,000	£990	£190	£90
£13,000	£1,075	£205	£95
£14,000	£1,155	£220	£105
£15,000	£1,240	£235	£110
£16,000	£1,320	£250	£120
£17,000	£1,405	£265	£125
£18,000	£1,485	£285	£135
£19,000	£1,570	£300	£140
£20,000	£1,650	£315	£150
Figures assume an after-tax return on savings of 2.5 per cent.			

Chapter 11

A child's own money

It is generally recognised that teaching children about money is a good thing – and the Government is so keen to encourage financial responsibility at a young age that it has made training in personal finance part of the National Curriculum. The Government also hopes to encourage the savings habit in future generations with the introduction of the Child Trust Fund (see Chapter 13), which is due to be introduced, sometime in 2005, for all children born since September 2002.

However, numerous surveys have shown that it is parents who are most influential in determining how well a child understands and handles money. Surveys also show that long-term financial habits are ingrained at an early age. This means that if parents don't initiate some kind of financial training before children get to secondary school – which is when formal lessons in personal finance typically start – they may already have developed bad financial habits that are difficult to shake off.

So what can parents do to prevent their offspring from growing into financially feckless adults? Although not guaranteed to make your children financially responsible, psychologists say that the main way in which parents can influence a child's attitude to money is by behaving in a financially responsible fashion themselves. There are also practical ways in which parents can teach their children how to handle and manage money including:

- giving them a regular income of their own in the form of pocket money (see page 137)
- developing the savings habit at an early age by helping them to open their own savings account (see page 138).

Pocket money

There are two main reasons for giving children a regular income of their own as soon as they can read, write and count. First, it helps them to develop a sense of financial independence (assuming that parents give up all control over how the money is spent). Second, handing over pocket money gives parents a self-defence mechanism against pester power, inasmuch as they can counter the 'can I have xyz?' question with the (possibly irritating) 'I don't know, how much pocket money have you got?' answer.

Opinion is divided over whether parents should give pocket money in return for a little light labour, or whether it is should be an unconditional handout. But whatever parents decide pocket money should depend on, there is a general view that, for children to learn useful lessons from having their own money to manage, parents should:

- pay a consistent amount of money on a regular basis – whether in cash or by standing order into a child's account – and pay it on time
- resist the temptation to top up pocket money or bail out a child out if he or she has blown it all on sweets by Saturday lunchtime
- let children spend their pocket money on whatever they choose, even if they do have a penchant for tacky tat
- give clear guidance on when children can expect pocket-money pay rises; typically this could be a child's birthday.

How much pocket money?

Setting levels of pocket money is not an exact science, since a lot will depend on how old your child is and on what you expect your child to finance out of his or her personal cash. It is fairly obvious, for example, that if you expect a teenager to pay their own mobile phone bill and buy their own clothes, you will need to pay more than if you intend pocket money to be used only for treats such as CDs and magazines.

However, as a guide, according to the annual Pocket Money Survey of 7 to 16-year-olds conducted by the Halifax in 2003, the average child receives around £6 a week. The research also revealed that while some parents get away with paying children in the 7-to-10 age group £2 a week, the majority of children of this age get £5 a week. Most children aged 11 to 16 receive between £5 and £10 a week, although the lucky few have managed to negotiate a weekly allowance of £20.

Developing the savings habit

Savers are made, not born, and, according to research by Abbey National, parental influence has a large part to play in shaping a

---

The world of work

Until a child becomes a teenager, the only ways in which he or she can legally earn money to top up parental handouts is by negotiating pay for doing jobs around the home. Employment outside the home for school-age children – which means under the school-leaving age of 16 – is strictly controlled under the Children and Young Persons Act 1933. This dictates the age at which school-age children can start working, the types of job they can do and the number of hours they can work. Depending on where you live, local-authority by-laws may impose further restrictions on the kind of work a teenager is allowed to do.

Although the law sets the minimum age at which a teenager can start working as 14, in some areas local-authority by-laws allow children of 13 to do certain sorts of jobs, such as taking on a paper round, serving in a shop or working in a hairdresser's, office, café or riding stables. Whatever the age of school-age workers, employers must register with the local authority and have a permit for each young person in their employment. If they don't, employers are breaking the law, as they are if they employ a child under 13 (or under 14 if a local authority does not permit employment of 13-year-olds).

By law, school-age workers can do only 'light' work, which rules out working in dangerous industries such as manufacturing, demolition, building or transport. Local-authority by-laws may also outlaw work that is considered unsuitable, such as working in a commercial kitchen, cinema, theatre, night club, betting shop or as a door-to-door salesperson. There are also restrictions on the number of hours that a

---

child's attitudes to saving. The research by Abbey National also found that the impact of parental influence extends to the way in which children save. Adults who were taught to save at an early age are more likely to save for the sake of it, as opposed to ring-fencing savings for a specific purpose. Early savers are also much less likely to borrow – preferring instead to save up for large items of expenditure.

So how can parents ensure that their children get into good financial habits? The most obvious way is to encourage children to open a child-friendly savings account (see page 140) once they are old enough to take an interest in having money. But developing

---

school-age worker can work. In addition, the law states that if a child is under 16, he or she cannot work:

- during school hours (taken to be 9.30 to 4.30 on weekdays)
- before 7am or after 7pm
- more than two hours on a school day
- more than one hour before school starts
- more than two hours on a Sunday
- for more than five hours (if under 15) or eight hours (if 15 or over) on Saturdays or on days in the school holidays
- for more than 35 hours a week in the holidays (25 hours a week if under 15).

The law also stipulates that a school-age worker who works in the holidays should have a minimum of two weeks off work at some point during the year.

If school-age workers' earnings – together with other taxable income such as interest on savings – exceed £4,615 (in the 2003–4 tax year), there will be income tax to pay at a rate of 10 per cent on the first £1,960 over £4,615, and then at a rate of 22 per cent on earnings over £6,575. But it is not until children are over the school-leaving age of 16 (whether still at school or not), that they become liable to pay National Insurance. However, National Insurance has to be paid only if weekly earnings exceed £89 week (in the 2003–4 tax year). At 18, young workers become entitled to the National Minimum Wage of £3.60 a week (£3.80 a week from October 2003).

good long-term saving habits may also require the use of various parental ploys such as:

- letting children choose, and operate, a savings account for themselves – which they can typically do from age seven – even if it does not pay the best rate of interest
- making them save up for must-have-but-not-strictly-necessary items out of their pocket money
- promising to match – or contribute a percentage of – any savings they make
- offering to split the cost of something a child wants if he or she saves up part of the cost
- helping children to set savings goals and rewarding them when each goal is met
- paying pocket money into a savings account rather than handing over cash.

TIP

If you are keen to teach your children about money, it is important that you let them make their own decisions about which savings account they open – and how many. If they display a healthy disregard for loyalty to a particular financial institution and open several accounts with the minimum amount necessary to get the freebies on offer, so be it. Similarly, it is helpful to let children make their own decisions about their dealings with banks and building societies. For example, if the counter staff at their chosen institution turns out to be unfriendly and uncooperative, children will soon learn to take their business to somewhere that offers more helpful service.

Choosing a children's savings account

Banks and building societies know that today's young savers are tomorrow's profitable adult customers, so they aim to catch them young. Some accounts try to capture young savers' attention with the offer of higher rates of interest than those paid on equivalent adult accounts, while others prefer to offer more tangible perks such as stickers, colouring books, money boxes, magazines, wallets and sports bags. Some child-specific accounts offer both.

CASE STUDY: Julia

Julia puts her savings habit – and the fact that she has always been careful with money – down to her Scottish parents. But Julia says that it wasn't until the birth of her daughter Florence – now four-and-a-half months old – that she really had a clear reason for saving. 'Before Florence was born, I just saved for the sake of it,' says Julia, 'but my financial focus has changed completely. Now I just want to save as much as I can for Florence's future.' The biggest priority for Julia and her husband Nicholas is saving to educate their daughter privately, but they also want to be able to finance Florence through university.

If you are helping a child to choose an account that he or she will operate – or will be in charge of on reaching age seven – the best way of finding a suitable account is to see what is available locally and let the child choose from what's on offer, even if this means not getting the best interest rate available.

However, parents who are in the happy position of having money to invest on behalf of a child who is not yet old enough to state a preference should choose an account purely on the interest rate. *Which?* publishes regular surveys of children's accounts, but you can also get up-to-date information on which children's accounts are paying the best rates of interest by consulting the specialist magazine *Moneyfacts*★ (published monthly), or by going to *www.moneyfacts.co.uk*. For more on building up a nest egg on behalf of a child, see Chapter 12.

TIP

Don't overlook what is on offer for children at local building societies, as these often pay better rates than children's accounts that are available nationally. For example, in May 2003 the best nationally available account was paying 4.25 per cent, while a higher rate of 4.7 per cent was available from a local building society which accepted deposits only from its local area.

The information published in *Money£acts* also gives details of which accounts offer cash cards. These can be useful for school-bound children who would otherwise only be able to obtain cash by visiting a branch at the weekend.

What not to choose

In the past, the savings accounts offered by National Savings & Investments (NS&I)* – as the former National Savings Bank is now called – were seen as a natural home for children's savings. However, the interest rate of 0.25 per cent paid on balances of up to £500 and 0.35 per cent on balances over £500 make the NS&I Ordinary Account one of the worst on the market. The Investment Account (which has a minimum investment of £20 and requires one month's notice of withdrawals) is not so bad, but the 2.2 per cent it pays on low balances does not compare favourably with rates of more than 4 per cent available from banks and building societies.

Youth accounts

Children who are under 18 cannot open an adult current account because they are not allowed credit in the form of an overdraft. But young people over 16 can get a taste of adult money management by opening one of the youth bank accounts on offer from high-street banks and a few building societies. These accounts do not pay great rates of interest – although the rates are typically better than on adult current accounts – but they do offer useful additional features such as:

- a debit card, which is useful for shopping online and for getting used to paying with plastic rather than cash
- the ability to pay by standing order and direct debit, which is essential for securing a good deal on a mobile-phone payment plan, for example.

Some accounts also provide a cheque book and most also offer the ability to manage the account by phone or over the Internet. More details of all the youth accounts are available in *Money£acts** or by going to *www.moneyfacts.co.uk*.

Opening an account

Children can usually open an account for themselves only from age seven, although a financial institution may be prepared to bend the rules if a child can reproduce his or her signature in a consistent fashion. To open an account for a child under seven in the child's name, you will need to provide proof of the child's identity in the form of any of the following in the child's name:

- birth certificate
- medical card
- passport
- rail or bus pass.

You will also need to provide proof of a child's address. If you share the same surname as your child, the proof of address should be a bank statement or utility bill (or similar) in your name. If you don't share the same surname as your child – or you are not the child's parent – ask the bank or building society what proof of the child's address it will accept. If you open an account in your child's name at your own bank or building society, you may not need to provide all the documents detailed above.

Teenagers opening a youth account will typically need to show something with their name, address and photograph on it, as well as a separate document confirming their address.

TIP

When opening an account for a child, make sure you register to have the interest paid without tax being deducted at source by completing form R85 (available from the bank or building society with which the account is to be held). Otherwise, in order to reclaim the tax that will be deducted it will be necessary to fill in a tax return on your child's behalf. Note that you should not complete form R85 if you are a parent who has paid money into an account in a child's name and the interest on it will exceed £100. (For more on this tax rule, see page 144.)

Children and tax

Children are potential taxpayers from the moment they are born, and as a result every child has his or her own personal allowance of £4,615 in the 2003–4 tax year, as well as the ability to make tax-free capital gains of £7,900.

In practice, most children are non-taxpayers – which means they can reclaim tax on interest from savings or register to have interest paid without tax being deducted (see page 143) – because their income is much less than their personal allowance. For example, to exceed his or her personal allowance of £4,615 a child would need to be earning interest on a lump sum of more than £100,000.

To stop parents avoiding paying tax by investing their own money in a child's name and so exploiting the fact that most children are non-taxpayers, interest earned on money given by parents is treated as theirs if it exceeds £100 per parent in any tax year. So this is unlikely to be a problem with savings accounts in which children stash their pocket money, since the limit of £100 will be breached only if a child has more than £2,500 to £3,000 in such an account. The same rule applies to interest earned on a cash Individual Savings Account which children over 16 can take out in their own name.

Interest earned on money given by people other than a child's parents is treated as the child's own and taxed accordingly.

TIP

It can make sense for a child to operate two savings accounts – one for pocket money from parents and another for birthday, Christmas and other money given by other generous relatives and friends, plus any earnings a child may have. It is also a good idea to ask relatives and friends who give large sums of money to accompany the gift by a letter making it clear that the money is a gift to the child.

Chapter 12

Building up a nest egg

Giving money to children by opening savings accounts for them is an excellent way of teaching them to become financially responsible (see Chapter 11). However, the problem with most savings accounts aimed at children is that the young account holders can usually get their hands on the money – and do what they like with it from age seven, since most banks and building societies will permit accounts for children to be opened only in a child's name. So if your aim is to build up a nest egg for a child for him or her to spend sometime in the future, a savings account may not be the most appropriate vehicle.

By contrast, other cash-based investments (see page 148) that are suitable for building up a nest egg make children wait until they are at least 16 before they can get hold of the cash. But if you would rather a child had to wait until he or she is 18 to be able to access the money you have built up, you can:

- invest in your own name and simply earmark your own savings to hand over to a child on his or her majority (see below)
- invest in shares or share-based investments (see page 152)
- set up a trust for the benefit of the child (see Chapter 13).

Another option, if you are planning for the really long term, is to pay into a pension on the child's behalf (see page 154), allowing him or her access to the money from age 50.

Should you invest in the child's name?

Not all investments allow you to invest in a child's name, although some let you 'designate' an investment as being intended for a child (see below). However, if you *can* put an investment in a child's name and you are not the child's parent, the advantage is that income earned by this money is treated as the child's. So there is no tax for you to pay on the income but a tax bill for the child only if:

- the total of all of a child's income – including earnings from part-time jobs and income from other investments – is greater than the child's personal tax allowance of £4,615 (in the 2003–4 tax year), or
- most of the income is from shares or other share-based investments (where tax is deducted before being paid and cannot be reclaimed).

However, this does not apply if the income earned by the investment is from money saved by a parent and the income earned on it exceeds £100 (or £200 if two parents invest jointly). In this case, the income is treated as the parent's for tax purposes and so is taxed at the parent's highest rate. But parents need to worry about going over the £100 limit only if they have more than £2,000 to £3,000 invested in their child's name.

Capital gains made by an investment are treated as the child's irrespective of who invested the money. This means that gains are tax-free provided they do not exceed £7,900 (in the 2003–4 tax year).

WARNING

The disadvantage of investing in a child's name is that you can't usually change your mind and take the money back. So if there is any chance that you might need access to the cash, it would be better to invest in your own name or simply designate an investment as being intended for a named child.

Designating investments for a child
If you want to keep your options open as to whether you or the child will eventually spend the nest egg you intend to build up, you can designate an investment in a child's name. This means that you hold the money in your own name, but add the child's name or initials.

This is simply a way of recording for your purposes the person to whom you intend to give the money; it does not give the child any legal rights to the money. Application forms for savings plans usually provide a space for adding this information, although not all savings institutions offer this facility. However, because you retain control over the money until you decide to hand it over to the child there are no tax advantages in designating an investment in a child's name.

Put yourself first

The golden rule when investing for children is not to commit any money to saving for a nest egg for them until you have sorted out your own finances. This means making sure that: you do not have expensive debts hanging over you, such as an overdraft or out-standing balance on a credit card; you have a cushion of cash to fall back on in emergencies; your family is adequately protected against the total or partial loss of your income by means of life and/or income-protection insurance (see Chapters 2 and 3); and your own financial future is secure by paying into a pension.

You should not feel guilty about putting your own finances first. Good financial advisers believe that getting your own finances on a firm footing means that you are in a much better position to help out your children financially than someone who ignores the basics.

Choosing investments for children

Choosing an investment for a child involves much the same principles as choosing an investment for yourself. You therefore need to take into account:

- how much you can afford to save
- how long you want to invest for
- how much risk you are prepared to take
- what the after-tax return on the investment is
- how flexible you want the investment to be.

Broadly, if there are fewer than five years to go until you want the child to have the nest egg and/or you don't want to take a risk with your money, cash-based investments are the most suitable way to save. However, if you can build up the nest egg over a longer period, investments linked to the stock market are an option. Stock-market investments carry the risk that you will get back less than you have invested, but they also have the potential to produce a bigger lump sum than you would get with cash-based investments – although this is not guaranteed.

If you want help choosing suitable stock-market linked investments for a child and/or you have a large lump sum to invest, you should consider using the services of an Independent Financial Adviser (IFA). To find an IFA, contact the Society of Financial Advisers★. IFA Promotion★ also gives information on finding an adviser.

TIP

The advantage of building up a nest egg through regular saving is that the regular 'gifts' you make to a savings plan intended for a child are exempt from inheritance tax. For more on gifts that do not attract inheritance tax, see Chapter 14.

Cash-based investments

If you want to keep your options open about whether your child will eventually receive the nest egg you are building up – therefore you simply earmark your own savings for that purpose – any of the savings products from banks, building societies and National Savings & Investments★ will be suitable. Details of savings products paying the best rates are published in the personal finance pages of the weekend press, or you can go to *www.moneyfacts.co.uk*. However, if you are happy to invest in a child's name, the options are:

- Children's Savings Accounts (see Chapter 11)
- Children's Bonus Bonds from National Savings & Investments★ (see page 149)
- Children's Savings Bonds from banks and building societies (see page 150).

> ### CASE STUDY: Arthur and Mary
>
> On the birth of each of their 11 grandchildren, Arthur and Mary set aside £1,000, which they will hand over as each grandchild reaches the age of 18. In the case of most of his grandchildren, Arthur has simply earmarked a portion of his investments in his stock-market-linked ISA (Individual Savings Account) to give to them when they become adults. But for two of his grandchildren he has invested in Children's Savings Bonds from a building society. This is partly because Arthur has been disappointed with the performance of the stock market in recent years and partly because he doesn't want the children's parents to be able to get at the money. By putting the bonds in his two grandchildren's names, Arthur and his wife will keep control over the money until the grandchildren reach their majority.

Children's Bonus Bonds

Issued by the Government-backed savings institution, National Savings & Investments* (NS&I), Children's Bonus Bonds offer a safe-as-houses home for a child's nest egg. They can be bought by anyone over the age of 16 for anyone under 16 and can be held until the holder reaches age 21 – although a child is free to cash in a bond once he or she reaches the age of 16. The minimum investment is £25 and the most you can invest in a single issue is £1,000 per child. You can invest more than £1,000 per child only when a new issue becomes available. This is decided by NS&I. The interest for each issue is fixed for five years at a time and it is tax-free. The sixth issue (current in May 2003) was paying a fixed rate of 3.5 per cent. At the end of each five-year term, you can leave the Bond earning a new tax-free rate of interest for a further five years. Children's Bonus Bonds are suitable for people who:

- are happy for a child to take control of the money at age 16
- can tie money up for five years at a time (a Bond can be cashed in before this, but will not accrue the maximum amount of interest)
- are parents, because the return is tax-free and so there is no risk of breaching the £100 tax rule (see page 146)

- want a fixed return that is guaranteed to be paid if the bond is held for the full five years
- do not want to take a risk with the money being invested for a child.

For more information on Children's Bonus Bonds, pick up a leaflet from the Post Office or go to the NS&I* website.

WARNING

If you are not the parent of a child, always consult the child's parents before investing in anything that has a limit on what can be paid into it to ensure that your gift does not take a child's investment over the limit. If this happens your money will have to be returned to you without interest. This applies to Children's Bonus Bonds (see page 149) from National Savings & Investments*, savings plans from friendly societies (see page 154) and stakeholder pensions (see page 154).

Children's Savings Bonds

The alternative to investing in a Children's Bonus Bond is to invest in a Savings Bond from a bank or building society. These work in much the same way as the Bonds from NS&I*, in that there is typically a fixed rate of interest that is guaranteed to be paid if you leave your money untouched for between three and five years. But unlike interest paid on Children's Bonus Bonds, the interest paid is not tax-free. However, if money is invested on behalf of a child by someone other than the parents, the interest will be tax-free provided that a child's total taxable income is less than his or her personal allowance of £4,615 (in the 2003–4 tax year). For grandparents and other generous adults, the advantage of investing in Savings Bonds from banks and building societies rather than in NS&I Children's Bonus Bonds is that the interest rates tend to be higher (see Table 12.1). You will find up-to-date information on Savings Bonds for children by consulting the latest edition of the specialist publication *MoneyFacts** (which is published monthly), or by going to *www.moneyfacts.co.uk*.

Table 12.1 Savings Bonds for children

Savings institution	Bond name	Term	Minimum investment	Maximum investment	Interest rate
Abbey National	Savings Bond	4 years	£500	£1,000	4%
Dunfermline Building Society	Children's Bond	3 years	£100	£1,000	4%
National Savings & Investments	Children's Bonus Bond	5 years	£25	£1,000	3.35%
NatWest Bank	Savings Bond	5 years	£1,000	£1,000	3.75%
Norwich & Peterborough Building Society	Loyalty Bond	5 years	£500	£1,000	4.4%

Source: Money£acts, May 2003.

WARNING

Do not invest in anything just because it has 'child', 'baby' or 'junior' or any other child-related word in its name. Many of the products that are marketed as child-friendly may offer very poor value and – because they are typically linked to investment-type life insurance – are usually quite inflexible if you have to stop saving.

A bit of fun

Strictly speaking, Premium Bonds from National Savings & Investments*, which can be bought for children by parents, guardians and grandparents, are a gamble rather than a proper investment. They should therefore be regarded as fun money, rather than as a way of building up a nest egg. However, they are less of a gamble than buying Lotto tickets, since you can at least get your money back if you don't win. If you like the idea of making a child or grandchild a potential millionaire, the minimum number of £1 Premium Bonds you can buy is 100, and the maximum is 30,000. For more information on how to buy Premium Bonds, pick up a free leaflet from the Post Office, or go to the website of National Savings & Investments* (where you can also check whether the Premium Bonds have won a prize).

Share-based investments

If you are prepared to take the risk that you may get back less than you have invested – a risk that may be worth taking if there are more than five years, although preferably more than ten, to go before the money you have saved for the benefit of your child will be used – investments linked to the stock market can be worth considering. Although there is no guarantee that history will repeat itself, investments linked to the stock market have traditionally produced higher returns than cash-based investments. Stock-market-linked investments also have the advantage that the money is unavailable to the child until he or she reaches the age of 18. The options available for investing on the stock market on behalf of children include:

- buying shares in individual companies (see below)
- investing in collective investments (see page 153)
- paying into a savings plan from a friendly society (see page 154)
- buying a child a stakeholder pension (see page 154).

Shares

Building up a nest egg by buying shares in individual companies is generally considered to be a very high-risk strategy, and so is not advisable unless you have large sums of money to invest and can spread the investment by buying shares in several different companies. However, as a fun investment, it can be worth buying shares in a company that the child has – or may develop – a particular interest in, such as the toy shop Hamleys, or one of the football clubs quoted on the Stock Exchange which include:

- Aston Villa
- Birmingham City
- Celtic
- Charlton Athletic
- Leeds United
- Manchester United
- Newcastle United
- Sheffield United
- Southampton
- Sunderland
- Tottenham Hotspur
- West Bromwich Albion.

To buy shares for children, you will first need to buy them in your name – and pay a dealing commission – and then transfer them into the child's name by completing a stock transfer form from the trustees of the company whose shares you have bought. There is no charge for this. However, the disadvantage of putting shares in a child's name is that the shares cannot be sold or transferred without a court order, as children cannot sell shares that they own until they are 18. The alternative is to transfer shares to a designated holding held in your name. You do this by filling in a stock transfer form and completing it with your name as both the transferor and transferee and specifying a designation – the child's initials, for example – in the transferee details. There is no charge for this sort of transfer.

CASE STUDY: Victoria

When her niece Claire was born, Victoria wanted to mark the birth with a financial gift. But Victoria didn't have much spare cash at the time – and didn't want to commit to a regular savings plan – so she transferred 100 of her shares in a demutualised building society into Claire's name by completing the stock transfer form that she got from the company's trustees. Although Claire officially owns the shares, she cannot sell them until she is 18, when Victoria is happy for Claire to do what she likes with the money. She did the same for her nephew Louis when he was born three years later.

Collective investments

While you need substantial amounts of money to invest seriously in the shares of individual companies, you can typically invest as little as £25 a month in collective investments – which include investment trusts, unit trusts and open-ended investment companies (OEICs) – where the money you invest is pooled with that of other investors and used to buy shares in a broad range of companies. Spreading your money over a large number of companies – typically between 50 and 100 – helps to reduce the risks associated with direct investment in shares, although it does not remove the risks altogether. There is still the risk that you will get back less than you invested, therefore you should consider investing in collective investments linked to the stock market only if you will be able to leave your money untouched for a minimum of five years.

You cannot usually invest in collective investments in a child's name, although most collective investment companies allow you to designate the investment in a child's name (see page 146).

You will find more information on investing in investment trusts on behalf of children in the free leaflet, *its for children*, from the Association of Investment Trust Companies★. For more information on using the other sorts of collective investments to build up a nest egg for a child, see the free leaflet, *A guide to investing on behalf of children through unit trusts and OEICs*, published by the Investment Management Association★, which also publishes *The Directory – a comprehensive list of unit trusts and OEICs*, a free guide giving useful comparative information on all the funds on the market. Comparative tables of some collective investments, showing the effect of the charges levied by collective investment companies, are also available on the website of the Financial Services Authority★.

Friendly Society savings plans

The apparent appeal of building up a nest egg by paying into a Friendly Society's insurance-based savings plan – many of which have child-related names – is that the return is completely tax-free whoever invests money on a child's behalf. However, the most you can invest per child is £25 a month or £270 a year, and you have to commit to saving for a minimum of ten years or risk getting back less than you have paid into the plan. A major disadvantage is that charges for these plans tend to be high, which can wipe out the benefit of receiving a tax-free return. You can compare the charges levied by Friendly Societies on their tax-free savings plans by using the comparative tables on the website of the Financial Services Authority★.

Stakeholder pensions

It's never too early to start planning for retirement and if you want to get a child's retirement fund off to a good start, consider investing in a stakeholder pension taken out in the child's name. The main advantage of investing in a pension on behalf of a child is that the Government adds basic-rate tax relief to the amount paid in. So in the 2003–4 tax year, for every £100 you invest, the Government adds £28 to the pension fund. But there are limits and the most you can pay into a pension on behalf of a child is £2,808 a year (£234 a month), which – once tax relief has been added – makes a total yearly contribution of £3,600. The main disadvantage of investing in a pension is that the earliest the 'child' will be able to get hold of the money is at age 50.

More information on stakeholder pensions is available from the Financial Services Authority*, which also publishes comparative tables of stakeholder products on its website.

Investing in the state pension

Once a child reaches 16, another way of improving a child's chances of a comfortable retirement is to 'invest' in the state pension on his or her behalf. You can do this by paying voluntary Class 3 National Insurance contributions for periods when they are not paying National Insurance themselves. This is particularly relevant to children over 16 who take a gap year and/or those studying at university, since taking time out of the world of work in these ways can leave gaps in a National Insurance record (although staying on into the sixth form doesn't). People who have gaps in their record may fail to qualify for certain state benefits or the basic state pension, or may receive only a reduced amount. You can fill in the gap at the time it is created, and you can also go back up to six tax years to fill earlier gaps in a National Insurance record. In the 2003–4 tax year, Class 3 National Insurance is paid at a flat rate of £6.95 a week. If you pay voluntary National Insurance on a regular basis, you can pay by quarterly bill or monthly by direct debit. Alternatively, you can pay lump sums by cheque or Internet transfer if you are making up for large gaps in a child's past record. For more information on paying voluntary National Insurance, consult the free leaflet, CA08 *Voluntary National Insurance contributions*, which is available from your local Tax Office or to download from the website of the Inland Revenue*.

Chapter 13

Giving money in trust

One of the problems with giving money directly to children is that – unless you choose investments which make the money inaccessible until they reach a certain age (see Chapter 12) – they can spend it as they wish. This may not bother you if the reason for giving is to encourage a child's sense of financial independence, but it can be a problem if you want a say in how the money is spent. The obvious way of making sure that you can dictate how money you have invested for your children is used is to invest on behalf of your children but in your own name. An alternative is to give money, property or other assets such as shares, to a trust that you set up for a child's (or children's) benefit.

Why give money in trust?

There are two main reasons why you might want to consider setting up a trust for your children or grandchildren. First, giving money in trust means that you can keep control of it until the children who stand to benefit from your gift reach an age when you would be happy for them to have the money – which, depending on the type of trust (see page 158), can be past the age of 18. Second, in most cases, money you give in trust no longer counts as part of your estate for the purposes of calculating inheritance tax. So gifts made in trust can reduce the amount of inheritance tax that your heirs may have to pay (see Chapter 14). Setting up a trust can also be a useful way of:

- saving income tax on income from investments and capital gains tax on gains made by the trust

- making financial provision for a child who is not good at handling money or one who is not able to look after his or her own financial affairs – because of a mental disability, for example
- giving to a group that is not yet complete – for example, you might want to make a gift to be shared by all your grandchildren, some of whom may not be born yet
- making a gift that is conditional on something happening at a future but as yet indeterminate date, such as birth or marriage
- keeping your gift a secret from the person who stands to benefit from it in the future.

The main disadvantage of giving money to a trust set up for the benefit of children is that once it is in place, you can't change your mind and get the money (or assets) back. Nor can you generally change your mind about the age at which the children will ultimately take control of the cash. Setting up and running a trust can also be expensive.

Trusts from the Government

In the future, all children will automatically have a trust set up for them by the Government under its plans for the Child Trust Fund. All children born on or after 1 September 2002 will benefit from the scheme, which is expected to go live sometime in 2005. All children will receive an initial payment of £250 on birth, but children from families who qualify for the full amount of Child Tax Credit (see Chapter 4) will get £500. Parents and other adults will be allowed to add up to £1,000 (in total) a year to the initial 'endowment' from the Government. It has been proposed that the Government will make further payments into the Child Trust Fund at certain key ages, but details had not been finalised at the time of writing. Children will be able to access the money in the fund at age 18, and there will be no restrictions on how the money can be used.

How trusts work

Trusts (also sometimes called 'settlements') are legal arrangements that enable you to give away money and assets while restricting and directing how and when they are used. Trusts can be used to make gifts in your lifetime and they can also be set up under the terms of a will. A trust involves three types of participant:

- the **settlor**, who is the person who gives away the assets that are placed in the trust and who decides the rules of the trust that are written in the trust deed, which is drawn up when the trust is set up. There can be more than one settlor – two grandparents, for example
- the **beneficiary**, who is the person who is to receive the assets or benefit from them. There are rules about when and how the benefit is to be received. There can be more than one beneficiary of a trust
- the **trustee** is the person – but, more usually, people – who looks after the assets placed in trust, and ensures that they are invested and used in accordance with the rules of the trust and with general trust law.

The settlor(s) can appoint themselves as trustees if they wish, and in the case of trusts set up for children, this is usually what happens. For more on what trustees do – and what is expected of them – see pages 168–9.

Types of trust

Which type of trust you choose will depend largely on when you want the children for whom you are setting a trust up to receive the money and how flexible you want the trust to be. There are several different types of trust, but the two that are generally considered to be most suitable for gifts to children are:

- **bare trusts**, which are the simplest – but least flexible – type of trust and the cheapest to set up (see page 159)
- **accumulation-and-maintenance trusts**, which may require the services of a solicitor or financial adviser to set up, but which are more flexible than bare trusts (see page 160).

The other types of trusts, both of which can also be set up under the terms of a will as a way of minimising inheritance tax on death, are:

- **discretionary trusts**, which are the most flexible types of trust (see page 161)
- **interest-in-possession trusts**, which allow you to control what happens to your assets from beyond the grave (see page 162).

Bare trusts

The simplest form of trust is a bare trust, also known as a 'simple' or 'absolute' trust. Bare trusts are suitable for people who:

- want to give money to a named child or children
- are confident that they will not change their minds about letting the named beneficiaries have the trust money
- are happy to let the beneficiaries take control of the money when they are 18.

The money in the trust is held in the name of a trustee – most commonly a parent or other relative – but the money and property held in the trust legally belongs to the child or children for whom the trust has been set up. If parents are trustees of a bare trust, they are allowed to use the income from the trust for 'the maintenance, education or benefit' of a child. So if the trust money is held in a

---

Designating investments for a child

A flexible (and cost-free) alternative to setting up a bare trust that allows you to keep control over money you want to give to a child – and also allows you to keep your options open as to whether you or the child will eventually spend it – is to put money into an account or savings plan 'designated' in the child's name. You hold the money in your own name but add the child's name or initials. This is simply a way of recording for your purposes the person to whom you intend to give the money; it does not give the child any legal rights to the money. Application forms for savings plans usually provide a space for adding this information, although not all savings institutions offer this facility. However, you retain control over the money (and pay any tax due on income from it) until you decide to hand it over to the child – which you can still choose not to do.

---

savings account, for example, the interest earned on the money could be used to pay for piano lessons or put towards school fees (see Chapter 6).

Advantages of bare trusts

The main advantage of setting up a bare trust is that it is cheap and simple and trustees do not have to fill in a separate tax return for the trust (as is the case with other sorts of trust – see page 169).

Disadvantages of bare trusts

The main disadvantage of using a bare trust to make gifts to children is that it is inflexible. Once a bare trust has been set up, you cannot change the beneficiary nor can you change the way the trust money is shared out if the trust has more than one beneficiary.

Accumulation-and-maintenance trusts

An accumulation-and-maintenance trust (which is a special type of discretionary trust – see page 161) is a more flexible alternative to a bare trust and is commonly used to put money into trust for children. Accumulation-and-maintenance trusts are suitable for people who:

- want to remain in control of the money put into the trust until they decide that the beneficiaries are old enough to use the trust money wisely
- are happy for the beneficiaries to receive income from the trust by the age of 25
- don't want to be too specific about which children will benefit from the trust
- want the trust to benefit children or grandchildren only.

Unlike a bare trust, the beneficiaries of an accumulation-and-maintenance trust do not have the absolute right to get their hands on the trust money at age 18 – although at least one must be allowed to have some or all of the income that has accumulated in the trust by the time they are 25 or reach the age specified by the settlor in the trust deed. The age at which they obtain the capital (that is, the money paid into the trust) can also be specified in the trust deed – and can be later than age 25 – or it can be left to the discretion of the trustees.

Income that is not accumulated in the trust to be paid out to the beneficiaries at a set age has to be used for the 'maintenance, education or benefit' of the children who stand to benefit from the trust money.

Advantages of accumulation-and-maintenance trusts

Apart from being able to restrict access to money in the trust beyond a child's eighteenth birthday, one of the main advantages of setting up an accumulation-and-maintenance trust is that it can be set up for the benefit of a specified group of children – including children who have not yet been born, but can be defined by their relationship to the settlor. For example, provided that grandparents have at least one grandchild when the accumulation-and-maintenance trust is set up, they can arrange it to benefit not only their existing grandchildren but also any future ones.

Disadvantages of accumulation-and-maintenance trusts

Depending on the type of investments held in trust, accumulation-and-maintenance trusts can be complicated and expensive to set up and administer. Unlike a bare trust, setting up an accumulation-and-maintenance trust requires professional help (see page 166). The trustees of an accumulation-and-maintenance trust are required to fill in a separate tax return for the trust and are responsible for paying tax on behalf of the trust (see page 169).

Discretionary trusts

A discretionary trust – also known as a 'flexible' trust – is the most suitable for people who want to be able to change their minds about:

- who will ultimately benefit from the trust
- at what age the beneficiaries will be able to get their hands on the money in the trust
- how much each beneficiary will receive from the trust.

Unlike an accumulation-and-maintenance trust, whether the beneficiaries of the trust receive any income from it is entirely at the discretion of the trustees, who may also be free to decide which beneficiaries get the capital with which the trust was set up. But how much discretion the trustees have depends on the wording of the trust deed.

Advantages of discretionary trusts

The main advantage of setting up a discretionary trust is the fact that it is very flexible. A discretionary trust also enables you (if you appoint yourself as a trustee) to retain control of money given to the trust until children reach whatever age you think reasonable for them to receive it. You can also set up a discretionary trust in your will, which can be useful if you need to make a will in a hurry – after the birth of a child, for example (see Chapter 1) – but don't have the time to think about who you would like to benefit from your wealth after your death.

Disadvantages of discretionary trusts

The main disadvantage of setting up a discretionary trust is that it can be very expensive both to set up and run. The trustees of a discretionary trust are also required to fill in a separate tax return for the trust and are responsible for paying tax on behalf of the trust (see page 169). Gifts to a discretionary trust also count as 'chargeable transfers' for inheritance tax purposes, which means that gifts to a discretionary trust may attract an inheritance tax bill at the time the gift is made. However, this is likely to happen only if the total of chargeable transfers made in a seven-year period amounts to £255,000 (in the 2003–4 tax year). The other disadvantage of a discretionary trust is that every ten years after the trust has been set up, inheritance tax at 20 per cent (half the usual rate of 40 per cent) is charged on the money held in trust. For more on inheritance tax, see Chapter 14.

Interest-in-possession trusts

Also known as 'fixed-interest' or 'life-interest' trusts, interest-in-possession trusts – which are typically set up in someone's will – have two different types of beneficiary:

- **life tenants** (called liferenters in Scotland), who are said to have a 'life interest' in the trust and who have the right to receive income earned by the trust money as the income arises, or to make use of property held by the trust – the right to live in a house, for example
- **capital beneficiaries** (also called 'remaindermen' and known as 'fiars' in Scotland), who are said to hold a 'reversionary interest' in the trust, which means that they have the right to receive

their share of the money placed in trust either on the death of the life tenants, or at a fixed date in the future, or when a specified event, such as a marriage, occurs.

Interest-in-possession trusts, which are less flexible than the other types of trust, are suitable for people who:

- have a clear idea of whom they want to benefit from the trust
- want to help two or more beneficiaries who have different financial needs
- eventually want to pass on assets to children or grandchildren, but need to provide for a partner or spouse in the meantime
- do not want the beneficiary to have full control of the assets in the trust or want to put off handing over control until a later date – until the beneficiary marries, for example, or graduates from university.

The beneficiaries who receive the income (or use of property) need not be the same as the beneficiaries who have the right to capital. For example, you might specify in your will that your share in the family home be put into trust, giving your spouse a life interest so that he or she could continue living there as long as desired, but giving the reversionary interest to your children so that they would inherit on the death of your spouse.

Advantages of interest-in-possession trusts

One of the main advantages of setting up an interest-in-possession trust is that you can control what happens to your possessions after your death, because a trust set up in a will cannot be varied in the same way that other instructions in a will can be (see Chapter 14). This can be particularly important if you have remarried but want your children to inherit your home rather than their step-parent, but would like your spouse to have the right to live in the home until his or her death.

Another advantage is that, although there may be an inheritance tax bill when the person who has a right to capital inherits the capital on the death of the life tenant, the capital does not attract inheritance tax if it is subsequently given away.

Disadvantages of interest-in-possession trusts

The main disadvantage of interest-in-possession trusts is that they are not as flexible as accumulation-and-maintenance trusts or discretionary trusts, because the beneficiaries have to be named at the outset. However, it is possible to set up a flexible interest-in-possession trust (or 'power-of-appointment' trust), where only the life tenants are named and the trustees are given discretion to decide who gets income and capital on the death of the life tenant(s). Interest-in-possession trusts can also be expensive and time-consuming to run, and the trustees are required to fill in a separate tax return for the trust and are responsible for paying tax on behalf of the trust (see page 169).

Tax and trusts

With a bare trust, if money in the trust was given by anyone other than a parent, the income earned on the money held in trust counts as the child's income, and will be taxed only if it exceeds the child's personal tax allowance of £4,615 (in the 2003–4 tax year), or if most of the income is from shares or other share-based investments (where tax is deducted before being paid and cannot be reclaimed). However, this does not apply if the money in a bare trust was given by a parent and the income earned on it exceeds £100 (or £200 if two parents each pay money into the trust). In this case, the income is treated as the parent's for tax purposes and so is taxed at the parent's highest rate.

Capital gains made by the trust are treated as the child's irrespective of where the money in the trust came from. This means that gains are tax-free provided they do not exceed £7,900 (in the 2003–4 tax year).

TIP

Parents considering setting up a trust for a child should consider investments which produce capital growth rather than income to make the most of the fact that the capital gains count as a child's and so are likely to be tax-free whereas, if more than £100, income counts as a parent's.

With the other types of trust, tax on income and capital gains produced by money held in trust is paid out of the trust fund by the trustees rather than by the beneficiaries of the trust. Gains made by

Table 13.1 Tax on trusts in the 2003–4 tax year

	Interest	Income from shares and share-based investments	Any other income	Capital gains [1]
Bare trusts	20%	10%	22%	20%
Accumulation-and-maintenance trusts	34%	25% [2]	34%	34%
Discretionary trusts	34%	25% [2]	34%	34%
Interest-in-possession trusts	20%	10%	22%	34%

[1] Rate is 0% if gains fall within the tax-free limit (see below).
[2] Rate is 34% for dividend income paid out of the trust.

trusts are tax-free if they do not exceed £3,950 (in the 2003–4 tax year). The rates of tax paid vary according to the type of income that the trust money produces and also on the type of trust. Table 13.1 shows the rates of tax applicable to income and gains retained in trusts in the 2003–4 year. The rates also apply to income paid out to beneficiaries, with the exception of discretionary trusts where dividend income paid out of the trust is taxed at 34 per cent.

With the exception of dividend income where tax cannot be reclaimed, with all types of trust the tax on income paid out of the trust *can* be reclaimed if the rate of tax paid by the beneficiaries (or their parents if the trust was set up by parents for the benefit of their own child and income exceeds £100) is lower than the rate of tax paid by the trust. Beneficiaries (or their parents) who are higher-rate taxpayers (unlikely in the case of young children) have to pay extra tax to make up the difference between a trust's tax rate and the higher rate of income tax of 40 per cent.

For more detailed information on the taxation of trusts, see the free leaflet, IR152 *Trusts An Introduction*, published by the Inland Revenue★ and available from the Self Assessment Orderline★ or from the Inland Revenue's website.

Inheritance tax and trusts

With the exception of gifts to discretionary trusts (see page 161), no inheritance tax is payable on gifts to trusts at the time that they are made because they are treated as potentially tax-free gifts. And no tax will have to be paid when the person who made the gift dies, provided that he or she lived for seven years after making the gift. Inheritance tax may have to be paid if a person dies within seven years of making a gift to a trust. Gifts to discretionary trusts set up for disabled people are also treated as potentially tax-free gifts for the purposes of inheritance tax. For more on inheritance tax, see Chapter 14.

How to set up a trust

When parents invest money which technically belongs to a child – a child receives a legacy from a grandparent, for example, or a compensation payment for an injury – on behalf of the child who is not yet old enough to invest the money, a bare trust is automatically set up.

However, to set up a bare trust with money given by the parent and held in the parent's name, it is sensible to formalise the trust by filling in a 'declaration of trust' form (which most savings providers will supply at no cost). Once completed, the form should be sent to the Inland Revenue with a cheque for £5 to cover the cost of the stamp duty charged by the Revenue for stamping the document.

Setting up other sorts of trusts can also be relatively straightforward if you are prepared to use the ready-made trust documents that some insurance and investment companies provide for free to use with their own investment products. However, going down this route may not be entirely cost-free, since some companies that provide ready-made trust documentation do not deal direct with the public, so it is necessary to use the services of an Independent Financial Adviser to get access to the ready-made trusts. The other disadvantage of using a ready-made trust is that they can be tied to investment products which may not be suitable for you. In addition, most companies advise you to have the trust checked out by a solicitor before committing yourself, for which you will have to pay a fee.

The reason for using a specialist solicitor with experience of setting up trusts to draw up a tailor-made trust deed for you is that the rules concerning trusts are extremely complicated – as are the tax rules. A solicitor can also advise on the type of trust that may be suitable for you and also on whether it is appropriate for you to set up a trust in your will (see Chapter 1). Solicitors will usually quote a fixed price for drawing up a trust deed, which typically costs around £500 for a straightforward trust, although a complex trust could cost a lot more.

Even if you already have a solicitor, because dealing with trusts is such a specialist area, it could be worth using a member of the Society of Trust and Estate Practitioners★ instead. Alternatively, the Law Society★ can provide names and addresses of solicitors with the necessary expertise in trusts. If you require investment advice as well as legal advice, you need to engage an Independent Financial Adviser, who may also be able to put you in contact with a suitably qualified solicitor. To find an Independent Financial Adviser, contact the Society of Financial Advisers★. IFA Promotion★ also provides information on finding an adviser.

Before a trust is set up

However you choose to set up a trust, it is helpful – and can save time and money – if you have a clear idea of what you want from the trust before meeting your adviser.

Before a trust deed can be drawn up, your adviser will need to know:

- your aims in setting up the trust
- what – and how much – you intend to give to the trust
- who is entitled to benefit from the trust – that is, who the beneficiaries are
- when income and capital are to be paid out
- who the trustees are
- what powers the trustees will have
- how you want the money held in the trust to be invested.

Unless you are setting up a trust in your will, it is quite normal to appoint yourself as the trustee of a trust that you are setting up for a child. However, from a practical point of view, it is common to have at least one other trustee. This can be your partner or spouse, although you should take advice on this because appointing a spouse as trustee can negate tax advantages. If you don't have a spouse or partner, you will need to find someone else to take on the sometimes onerous job of being a trustee.

Anyone over 18 can be a trustee, even someone who has been bankrupt or has been convicted of a serious crime. Beneficiaries can be trustees, though usually this is not a good idea as trustees should not normally profit from a trust and should be wary of acting if they have a conflict of interest. You cannot force someone to be a trustee, but once someone has taken on the job, he or she does not have an automatic right to resign.

What trustees do

The only duties that the trustees of a bare trust have to perform is to invest the money entrusted to them on behalf of a child or children, monitor the investment and hand it over to the named beneficiaries of the trust when they reach the age of 18 (or marry if this happens earlier), which is when the beneficiaries become absolutely entitled to the money and/or property held in trust.

The duties and powers of trustees of other types of trust are set out in various Acts of Parliament, although some of a trustee's statutory duties and powers may be overridden by what it says in the trust deed. Among other things, the rules say that trustees have a duty to:

- read and understand the trust deed
- comply with the terms of the trust as set out in the trust deed
- know where all the assets of the trust are kept
- keep a check on the actions of other trustees and make sure that they keep to the rules of the trust
- take reasonable care in carrying out their powers and duties
- ensure that the right people get the right trust assets
- ensure fairness between beneficiaries
- provide beneficiaries with information about the trust and its investments if they ask
- take action only if all trustees have agreed unanimously on a particular course of action, unless the trust deed says that majority voting is allowed
- take professional investment advice where appropriate
- get the best price for any assets that they choose to sell
- account for and pay tax on the trust to the Inland Revenue.

The rules say that trustees typically have the power to:

- hand over trust money to a beneficiary
- use the income of the trust for the maintenance, education or benefit of a beneficiary

- set reasonable expenses against the money in the trust
- delegate administrative tasks, such as dealing with paperwork, managing investments, keeping assets safe and so on
- invest in a way that is suitable for the aims of the trust
- sell trust property.

After a trust has been set up

After you have set up a trust (other than a bare trust – see page 159), you should inform the nearest Inland Revenue Trusts* office to where you live that you have put property into trust. If you expect the trust to produce income and/or capital gains, you (or one of the trustees) should complete form 41G(Trust) and send it to the Inland Revenue Trusts* office nearest to your home.

In addition, you – or another trustee – will be expected to fill in a self-assessment tax return for the trust each year and pay the tax owed by the trust. For more detailed information on the dealings that the trustees must have with the Inland Revenue, see the free leaflet, IR152 *Trusts An Introduction*, published by the Inland Revenue* and available from the Self Assessment Orderline* or from the Inland Revenue's website.

Chapter 14

Tax on gifts to children

It may seem an odd concept that financial gifts to children attract tax at all – but they do. Inheritance tax is the main tax on gifts of cash, shares, property and other valuable assets, and it may be charged both on gifts you make when you are still alive and on those you leave on death. So unless they are the kind of gifts that are exempt from inheritance tax (see page 171), all other gifts to children – whether they are from parents, grandparents, or other generous relatives – carry a potential inheritance tax bill.

However, it is not the person who makes a gift who has to pay the tax, because inheritance tax is not paid until after a person's death (and you can't pay tax from beyond the grave). But, as far as taxing gifts to children goes, there is one exception to the only-charged-on-death rule. If you give money to a child (or children) through a discretionary trust, there *may* be an immediate inheritance tax bill (see Chapter 13).

The other tax on gifts

While most gifts you make while you are alive currently escape an immediate inheritance tax bill, they may not escape a bill for capital gains tax, which is a tax on the increase in the value of certain assets. Cash gifts (made in sterling) do not attract capital gains tax. But if you give away assets – such as shares, unit trusts and property – and the increase in value is more than £7,900 (for gifts made in the 2003–4 tax year), you (rather than the recipient) could face a capital gains tax bill.

On death, inheritance tax is automatically payable by your heirs only if what you leave on death (called your 'estate') is valued for inheritance tax purposes at more than £255,000 (for deaths occurring in the 2003–4 tax year). Tax is charged at 40 per cent on any amount over £255,000 (but see page 172, for when a lower rate of inheritance tax may be charged). For more on inheritance tax on death, and the steps you can take to minimise the tax that the people who inherit from you might have to pay, see pages 177–80.

Tax-free gifts to children

There is no tax to pay on gifts that are exempt from inheritance tax. The exemptions that are particularly relevant to gifts to children are:

- **regular gifts** of any amount that are part of your normal expenditure provided your standard of living does not suffer as a result of making the gifts and provided there is a regular pattern of giving (to the same recipient). So paying a monthly amount into a savings plan would count as a tax-exempt regular gift, as would paying termly school fees for a grandchild or giving a yearly birthday cheque
- **gifts for education, training or maintenance** of your children (including adopted children and children you look after as their guardian) if they are still in full-time education or training or they are aged 18 or under
- **small gifts** worth up to £250 a year to each recipient. There's no limit on the number of people to whom you can give this category of tax-free gifts

But this applies only to gifts made when you are alive. To avoid double taxation, gifts you leave after death are not subject to capital gains tax – although if inherited assets are subsequently sold, any gains made may be liable for this tax. To find out more about capital gains tax on gifts, ask the Self Assessment Orderline* for the free leaflet, CGT1 *Capital gains tax – an introduction*, which is also available on the Inland Revenue website*. For how income tax affects gifts to children – and who has to pay it – see page 146.

- **wedding gifts** of up to £5,000 if given by the parents of the bride and groom, of up to £2,500 if given by the couple's grandparents (or great-grandparents), and of up to £1,000 if given by anyone else, whether or not they are related to the couple.

In addition to these tax-free gifts, you can also give away up to a total of gifts worth £3,000 each tax year to anyone. If you use the full £3,000 in a tax year, you can carry it forward to the next tax year and give up to £6,000 (that is, two lots of £3,000). But the limit can be carried forward for one tax year only

Potentially tax-free gifts to children

With the exception of gifts to a discretionary trust (see Chapter 13), all other gifts to children are treated for tax purposes as 'potentially exempt transfers'. This means that there is no inheritance tax to pay at the time you make the gift and no tax for your heirs to pay on your death *unless* you die within seven years of making the gift.

If death occurs before seven years have elapsed after making a potentially tax-free gift, the total amount of all gifts of this kind made in the seven years before death are added to your estate and taxed accordingly (see page 173). However, tax on the potentially exempt transfers added to your estate may not be charged at the full rate of inheritance tax (40 per cent in the 2003–4 tax year) if they were made more than three years before death. In this case, the tax is reduced on a sliding scale.

To find out more about tax on potentially exempt transfers, ask the Inheritance Tax Helpline★ for the free leaflet, IHT2 *Inheritance tax on lifetime gifts*, which is also available on the Inland Revenue website★. The leaflet, IR295 *Relief for gifts and similar transactions* gives details of how the sliding scale works for tax on gifts made more than three years before death.

Inheritance tax on death

On death, the whole of your estate – roughly speaking, what you own when you die plus any potentially tax-free gifts made in the seven years before death – is treated as your final gift. There is no inheritance tax to pay if your husband or wife inherits your whole estate, because all gifts to a spouse (both in life and on death) are exempt from inheritance tax. There may be a tax bill if your spouse will inherit only part of your estate, because gifts (in the form of bequests in your will) to anyone else – including children and a partner to whom you were not married – are taxable. But whether there will be a tax bill or not depends on the value of your estate.

For a rough idea of whether your heirs face a potential inheritance tax bill, add up:

- the total of all gifts you have made in the last seven years which were not tax free (so do not include any of the type listed on page 171)
- the value of your property – including foreign property – or your share of property owned jointly
- cash, savings and investments
- the proceeds of any insurance policies which would pay out on your death and which have not been written in trust (see Chapter 2)
- property held in a trust from which you are entitled to income (see Chapter 13).

From that total, subtract:

- any debts which would not be cleared on your death (for example, if you have not taken out life insurance to cover your mortgage, or you have an outstanding balance on your credit card)
- gifts which are tax-free on death, such as those to a spouse (but not an unmarried partner) and to charities
- an estimate of the cost of your funeral, which is typically around £3,000.

If the figure you end up with is less than £255,000, it falls within what is called the 'nil-rate band' for inheritance tax, and your heirs would not face an inheritance tax bill if you died in the 2003–4 tax year. However, even though the nil-rate band is usually increased at least in line with inflation each year, it is worth reviewing the value of your estate, particularly any property you own, on a regular basis.

If your estate is worth more than £255,000, your heirs face a potential tax bill of 40 per cent of the amount over the nil-rate band.

So if you reckon your estate is worth £300,000, there would be tax to pay on £45,000 (£300,000 minus £255,000) and the tax bill would be £18,000 (40 per cent of £45,000).

You will find more detailed information on working out an inheritance tax bill in the free leaflet, IHT15 *Inheritance tax – how to calculate the liability*, available from the Inheritance Tax Helpline★ and also on the Inland Revenue★ website.

Who pays the inheritance tax?

In general, any inheritance tax due – which has to be paid before probate is granted and your estate distributed – is deducted from your estate. However, the recipient of an individual gift will be expected to pay the tax due on it if:

- your will (if you have one) specifies that a bequest is to 'bear its own tax'
- tax becomes due on what was a potentially exempt gift (see page 172), because it was made less than seven years before the death (although your estate will be billed if the recipient is unwilling or unable to pay).

How to plan to pay for an inheritance tax bill

The requirement to pay inheritance tax before probate is granted – and so before money and assets in your estate are released – can cause problems if you leave an unmarried partner and/or children and they do not have the cash to pay the tax bill, and may therefore need to borrow to pay the bill. It is a particular problem if your biggest asset is your home and it would have to be sold to meet the inheritance tax bill. Table 14.1 shows how much your heirs might have to pay if you died in the 2003–4 tax year.

Insurance against a future tax bill

If you want to make sure that your heirs have sufficient cash to pay an inheritance tax bill, one solution is to buy a life-insurance policy and have it written in trust for your beneficiaries so that the cash does not form part of your estate (see Chapter 1). Buying life insurance also has the advantage that the premiums you pay for it count

Table 14.1 How much inheritance tax?

Taxable value of estate	Potential tax bill
£250,000	£0
£300,000	£18,000
£350,000	£38,000
£400,000	£58,000
£450,000	£78,000
£500,000	£98,000
£750,000	£198,000
£1,000,000	£298,000
Figures are for the 2003–4 tax year.	

as regular gifts (see page 171) and so are free from inheritance tax. The most suitable form of life insurance for paying the tax is:

- **term insurance** with a seven-year term if you just want to provide cash for the bill on a potentially tax-free gift (which otherwise the recipient would have to pay)
- **whole-life insurance,** which has no fixed term if you want to cover the tax on your whole estate or just one asset such as the family home. Married couples should buy a joint-life policy that pays out after the second death, while partners who are not married should buy a policy each (assuming there is a potential inheritance tax bill on each partner's death).

You can buy term insurance purely on price and you will find up-to-date information on companies offering the cheapest deals in the tables published in the personal finance pages of the national press. Alternatively, go to *www.moneyfacts.co.uk*. Whole-life insurance has an investment element, so it is wise to get help choosing a policy by using the services of an Independent Financial Adviser. To find one, contact the Society of Financial Advisers★. IFA Promotion★ also provides information on finding an adviser.

Where to keep cash for a future tax bill
An alternative solution is to build up enough cash to meet the inheritance tax in a savings account with a bank or building society that

participates in the Government-backed streamlined inheritance tax scheme. This allows cash from a dead person's current or savings account to be used to pay a tax bill directly to the Inland Revenue *before* probate is granted. You can also pay tax before probate is granted with savings accounts, bonds and certificates from National Savings and Investments★ and also Government Stock (also called gilts) held on the Bank of England Registrar's Department★.

For more information, see the free leaflet, IHT11 *Payment of Inheritance Tax from National Savings or from British Government stock on the Bank of England Register*, which is available from the Inheritance Tax Helpline★ and also on the Inland Revenue★ website.

Business benefits

If your children (or partner) inherit your business, in most cases no inheritance tax (or a reduced amount) has to be paid. This is because, unless the business is wholly or mainly an investment business, it will qualify for business property relief of up to 100 per cent. You will find more detailed information on inheritance tax relief for businesses in the free leaflet, IHT17 *Inheritance tax: Businesses, farms and woodlands*, available from the Inheritance Tax Helpline* and also on the Inland Revenue* website.

Inheritance tax planning

The golden rules in inheritance tax planning are: don't do anything that would put your financial security – or that of your partner – at risk; and don't do anything you cannot afford to do. Risking your own financial security just to give your children slightly more than they would otherwise inherit is not a good idea. Also, since it is possible to reduce an inheritance tax bill after death by rearranging a will (see page 179), planning may not be essential, especially if you are married and plan to leave everything to your other half. However, not doing anything can cause problems if – as might be the case for unmarried partners whose home is their biggest asset – a family home would have to be sold to meet an inheritance tax bill.

How to minimise a potential inheritance tax bill

Inheritance tax planning is often associated with devilishly complex tax-avoidance schemes, but in fact there are several fairly simple ways in which you can reduce a potential inheritance tax bill that are outlined below.

Give away your wealth before you die

The main way of reducing a potential inheritance tax bill is by giving away your worldly wealth before you die – sometimes called 'estate spreading'. This makes sense only if you can afford to give away money without jeopardising your financial security. If you can afford to make gifts now and would like to see the recipient enjoying your generosity:

- make full use of tax-free gifts, in particular the annual exemption of £3,000 and the tax-free status of regular gifts out of income (see page 171)
- make gifts sooner rather than later if your gifts will total more than the nil-rate band of £255,000 (in the 2003–4 tax year) over the next seven years. If you survive for three years after making the gift, the tax is reduced on a sliding scale, and if you survive for seven years there is no tax at all (see page 172)
- watch out for capital gains tax on lifetime gifts. Gifts of cash and certain other assets are not liable to the tax, but gifts of things like shares, holiday homes and valuables to anyone other than your spouse may mean a capital gains tax bill (see page 170).

If you would like to give to your children or grandchildren but prefer to retain control over the money until they reach a certain

---

WARNING

You cannot avoid inheritance tax by giving away something that you continue to benefit from – if you give your children your house, for example, but continue to live in it rent free. This is called making a gift 'with reservation', and this type of gift still counts as part of your estate for the purposes of calculating inheritance tax.

age, consider setting up a trust. This removes money from your estate for inheritance tax purposes, but enables you to keep control over the money (see Chapter 13).

Make a will

Making a will is the best way to make sure that your worldly goods end up where you want them to after your death. If you don't leave a valid will, the intestacy rules distribute them in ways that might not be what you intended. For example, if you live with someone without being married to him or her, he or she might get nothing (for more on the importance of making a will, see Chapter 1).

If you are not sure what to do with the whole or part of your estate, you can set up a discretionary trust in your will, giving the trustees two years to give away the property. You can discuss your wishes with the trustees so that they know the priorities you would set; and if they make the gifts within the two years, the tax is the same as if you had made the gifts yourself. For more on setting up a trust, see Chapter 13.

If you are married, a will can also be used as a tax-saving tool if you are prepared not to leave everything to your spouse. If your spouse genuinely could manage without inheriting your whole estate, married couples should consider making gifts in their will to children and grandchildren up to the level of the nil-rate band of £255,000 (in the 2003–4 tax year). This is not a tax-saving option open to lone or unmarried parents.

WARNING

It is very important to decide who will be responsible for paying the tax if you decide to leave part of your estate to your children or grandchildren and the rest to your spouse. Unless your will says that the gifts to your children are to bear their own tax, the tax on them will normally come out of what remains of the estate after the gifts have been made. If you've left the remainder to your spouse, much (or all) of it could be swallowed up in paying the tax on the gifts for your children or grandchildren.

Change the way you own your home

If you are part of a couple and own your home as joint tenants, both partners own the whole home and if one dies, their share automatically goes to the other, and can't be given to anyone else – even if a will says something different. It still forms part of your estate for tax purposes, so there could be tax to pay if the other joint tenant is not the wife or husband. If the joint tenants are married, there'll be no tax on the first death, but the whole value of the house would be in the estate when the second partner dies.

It is also possible to own property as tenants in common, where each person owns part of the asset separately and can decide to whom their portion is left. If you are married, you could save inheritance tax by leaving your share of the house to your children rather than to your spouse. A solicitor can advise on changing the way in which you own a home, but bear in mind that leaving half the family home to your children could endanger the right of the surviving spouse to live in it after your death. It is not unheard of for cash-strapped offspring to force the sale of a family home.

How to minimise inheritance tax after death

After someone's death, his or her will can currently be rearranged by drawing up a deed of variation. This sets out how you want the gifts to be changed. The revised gifts take effect for inheritance tax just as if they had actually been made by the person who drew up the original will. So rearranging a will after someone's death (or creating one if there was no will – see Chapter 1) can save inheritance tax. The rules for varying a will say that:

- the new arrangements must take effect within two years of the person's death
- the arrangements must have the consent of all beneficiaries under the will who are affected by them.

Note that if a parent varies a will and redirects a legacy producing income of more than £100 a year to his or her unmarried child under 18, the income is taxed as the parent's until the child reaches 18 or marries.

To find a solicitor to draw up a deed of variation, contact the Society of Trust and Estate Practitioners★ or the Law Society★. For more information on the tax implications of varying a will after someone's death, see the free leaflet, IHT8 *Alterations to an inheritance following a death*, available from the Inheritance Tax Helpline★ and also on the Inland Revenue★ website.

How to get help with minimising inheritance tax

If you plan to save your heirs inheritance tax by making small gifts up to the £3,000 limit (see page 172), you are unlikely to need professional help, although you should use a solicitor to draw up your will (if you don't already have one).

In most other cases, you should consult a solicitor before doing anything that involves changing or giving away ownership of major assets such as your home. Even if you already have a solicitor, because dealing with estates is a specialist area, it could be worth using a member of the Society of Trust and Estate Practitioners★ instead. Alternatively, the Law Society★ can provide names and addresses of solicitors with the necessary expertise both in wills and trusts. An independent adviser can also advise on inheritance tax planning. To find one, contact the Society of Financial Advisers★. IFA Promotion★ also provides information on finding an adviser.

The Which? Guide to Giving and Inheriting, published by Which? Books★, gives information on tax-efficient ways of passing on money, property and other valuables.

Addresses and websites

Abbey National
Tel: (0800) 555 100
Website: www.abbeynational.co.uk

ACAS Helpline
Tel: (08457) 474747
For information on employment rights for working parents

Advisory Centre for Education
1c Aberdeen Studios
22 Highbury Grove
London N5 2DQ
Helpline: (0808) 800 5793
(2pm–5pm weekdays)
Exclusion Helpline: (0808) 800 0327
(2pm–5pm weekdays)
Fax: 020-7354 9069
Email: ace-ed@easynet.co.uk
(for people unable to use the telephone advice line because of a disability)
Website: www.ace-ed.org.uk
Advisory service for the state sector

Association of Investment Trust Companies
Durrant House
8-13 Chiswell Street
London EC1Y 4YY
Tel: 020-7282 5555
Fax: 020-7282 5556
Email: enquiries@aitc.co.uk
Website: www.itsonline.co.uk

Association of Tutors
Sunnycroft
63 King Edward Road
Northampton NN1 5LY
Tel: (01604) 624171
Fax: (01604) 624718
Website: www.tutor.co.uk

Bank of England Registrar's Department
Southgate House
Southgate Street
Gloucester GL1 1UW
Tel: (01452) 398080
Fax: (01452) 398098
Website: www.bankofengland.co.uk

Bank of Scotland Mortgages
Tel: (0845) 603 1136
Website: www.bankofscotland.co.uk

Benefit Enquiry Line
Tel: (0800) 882 200
Website: www.dwp.gov.uk
To find out which state benefits you might be entitled to when ill, disabled or are a carer. Contact your local office for details regarding benefits when unemployed

The Boarding Schools' Association
Grosvenor Gardens House
35-37 Grosvenor Gardens
London SW1W 0BS
Tel: 020-7798 1580
Fax: 020-7798 1581
Email: bsa@iscis.uk.net
Website: www.boarding.org.uk

Boots
Tel: (0845) 840 2020
Website: www.bootsinsurance.com

Campus Insurance
Tel: (0800) 083 3204
Website: www.cover4students.co.uk

Charcol Mortgage Brokers
Tel: (0800) 718191
Website: www.charcolonline.co.uk

Chase de Vere Mortgage Management
Tel: (0800) 358 5533
Website: www.cdvmm.com

Child Benefit Office
Inland Revenue – Child Benefit
Office
Washington
Newcastle upon Tyne NE88 1ZB
Tel: (0845) 302 1444
Email: child.benefit@ir.gsi.gov.uk
Website: www.inlandrevenue.gov.uk

Child Benefit Office (Northern Ireland)
Windsor House
9-15 Bedford Street
Belfast BT2 7EU
Tel: 028-9054 9000
Email: child.benefit@ir.gsi.gov.uk
Website: www.inlandrevenue.gov.uk

ChildcareLink
Tel: (0800) 096 0296
Website: www.childcarelink.gov.uk
Government-sponsored service providing
information on childcare together with
details of local Children's Information
Services which can provide face-to-face or
telephone advice on all aspects of childcare

Child Support Agency
Enquiry Line: (0845) 713 3133
(8am–8pm weekdays, 8.30am–5pm
Sat)
Email: csa-nel@dwp.gsi.gov.uk
Website: www.csa.gov.uk

Child Support Agency (Northern Ireland)
Enquiry Line: (08457) 139896
(8am–8pm weekdays, 9am–5pm Sat)
Email: belfast-cust-helpline@
dwp.gsi.gov.uk
Website: www.dsdni.gov.uk

The Choir Schools' Association
CSA Bursary Trust
The Minster School
Deangate
York YO1 7JA
Tel: (01904) 624900
Website: www.choirschools.org.uk

Citizens' Advice Bureaux
Website: www.citizensadvice.org.uk

Club Direct
Tel: (0800) 083 2466
Website: www.clubdirect.com

Community Legal Service
Directory line: (0845) 608 1122
Website: www.justask.org.uk

Community Service Volunteers
237 Pentonville Road
London N1 9NJ
Tel: 020-7278 6601
Email: information@csv.org.uk
Website: www.csv.org.uk

CostOut.co.uk
Website: www.costout.co.uk

Daycare Trust
21 St George's Road
London SE1 6ES
Tel: 020-7840 3350
(10am–5pm weekdays)
Fax: 020-7840 3355
Email: info@daycaretrust.org.uk
Website: www.daycaretrust.org.uk

Department for Education and Skills
Information Line: (0800) 731 9133
Website: www.dfes.gov.uk

**Department for Education and Skills
Music and Dance Scheme Team**
Mowden Hall
Staindrop Road
Darlington DL3 9BG
Tel: (01325) 391181
Email: paul.zeltins@dfes.gsi.gov.uk
Website: www.dfes.gov.uk/mds

**Department for Education and Skills
Pupil Wellbeing and Transport Team**
Mowden Hall
Staindrop Road
Darlington DL3 9BG
Tel: (01325) 391272
Fax: (01325) 392 040
Email:
pwtt.well-being@dfes.gsi.gov.uk
Website: www.dfes.gov.uk

**Department for Work and Pensions
(DWP)**
Public enquiry office
Tel: 020-7712 2171
Fax: 020-7712 2386
Website: www.dwp.gov.uk
*For general enquiries, contact your local
benefits office*

**Department of Health (Northern
Ireland)**
Social Services and Public Safety
Human Resources Directorate
Room 3
Dundonald House
Upper Newtownards Road
Belfast BT4 3SF
Tel: 028-9052 4746
*For details of NHS bursaries in Northern
Ireland for students training to be
healthcare professionals*

Department of Trade and Industry
Publications Orderline:
0870 150 2500
Website: www.dti.gov.uk

Direct Line
Tel: (0845) 2460 489
Website: www.directline.com

Directory of Social Change
Customer Service/Publications
Department
24 Stephenson Way
London NW1 2DP
Tel: 020-7209 5151
Fax: 020-7391 4804
Email: books@dsc.org.uk
Website: www.dsc.org.uk

Dudley Building Society
Tel: (01384) 231414
Website:
www.dudleybuildingsociety.co.uk

Education Otherwise
PO Box 7420
London N9 9SG
Tel: 0870 730 0074
(10am–8pm weekdays)
Email:
enquiries@education-otherwise.org
Website:
www.education-otherwise.org
For information on educating children at home

Employment Agency Standards
Helpline: (0845) 955 5105
Website:
www.dti.gov.uk/er/agency-kyr.html
The helpline provides a free and confidential complaints service about agency conduct and will investigate any complaints made by families or nannies

Endsleigh Insurance
Tel: (0800) 028 3571
Website: www.endsleigh.co.uk

Family Mediation Scotland
18 York Place
Edinburgh EH1 3EP
Tel: 0131-558 9898
Fax: 0131-558 9831
Email:
info@familymediationscotland.org.uk
Website:
www.familymediationscotland.org.uk

The Family Mediators' Association
Grove House
Grove Road
Redland
Bristol BS6 6UN
Tel: 0117-946 7180
Email: info@fmassoc.co.uk
Website: www.fmassoc.co.uk

Financial Services Authority
25 The North Colonnade
Canary Wharf
London E14 5HS
Tel: (0845) 606 1234
Fax: 020-7676 1099
Email: consumerhelp@fsa.gov.uk
Website: www.fsa.gov.uk

Financial Times
Financial Times Business Ltd
Tabernacle Court
16-28 Tabernacle Street
London EC2A 4DD
Tel: 020-7382 8000
Website: www.ft.com

Flexicover direct
Tel: (0800) 783 8338
Website: www.flexicover.co.uk

gapyear.com
Website: www.gapyear.com

The Gap-Year Guide Book
Website: www.gap-year.com

Go Travel Insurance
Tel: 0870 243 6006
Website:
www.gotravelinsurance.co.uk

The Grants Register
Palgrave MacMillan
Houndmills
Basingstoke
Hampshire RG21 6XS
Tel: (01256) 329 242
Fax: (01256) 479 476
Email: bookenquiries@palgrave.com
Website: www.palgrave.com

Guardian's Allowance Unit
PO Box 1
Newcastle upon Tyne NE88 1AA
Tel: (0845) 302 1464
Email: child.benefit@ir.gsi.gov.uk
Website: www.inlandrevenue.gov.uk

Halifax
Tel: (08457) 273747
Website: www.halifax.co.uk

Housing Corporation
Maple House
149 Tottenham Court Road
London W1T 7BN
Tel: 020-7393 2000
Fax: 020-7393 2111
Email:
enquiries@housingcorp.gsx.gov.uk
Website: www.housingcorp.gov.uk

IFA Promotion
2nd Floor
117 Farringdon Road
London EC1R 3BX
Tel: (0800) 085 3250
Website: www.unbiased.co.uk

Immigration and Nationality Directorate
Lunar House
40 Wellesley Road
Croydon
Surrey CR9 2BY
Tel: (0870) 606 7766
Website:
www.ind.homeoffice.gov.uk
For advice on visas for au pairs from outside the European Union

Independent Schools Council information service (ISCis)
Grosvenor Gardens House
35-37 Grosvenor Gardens
London SW1W 0BS
Tel: 020-7798 1500
Fax: 020-7798 1531
Email: info@iscis.uk.net
Website: www.iscis.uk.net

Inheritance Tax Helpline
Tel: (0845) 302 0900

Inland Revenue
Tel: 020-7667 4001
Website: www.inlandrevenue.gov.uk

Inland Revenue New Employers' Helpline
Tel: (0845) 607 0143

Inland Revenue Trusts (Greater London)
Charles House
375 Kensington High Street
London W14 8QS
Tel: 020-7605 9933
Fax: 020-7371 2124

Inland Revenue Trusts (Greater Manchester)
Albert Bridge House
1 Bridge Street
Manchester M60 9AF
Tel: (0161) 288 6747
Fax: (0161) 288 6701

Inland Revenue Trusts (Scotland)
Meldrum House
15 Drumsheugh Gardens
Edinburgh EH3 7UL
Tel: 0131-777 4343
Fax: 0131-777 4035

Inland Revenue Trusts (South West England)
Lysnoweth
Infirmary Hill
Truro
Cornwall TR1 2JD
Tel: (01872) 245403
Fax: (01872) 245315

Inland Revenue Trusts (rest of the United Kingdom)
Huntingdon Court
90-94 Mansfield Road
Nottingham NG1 3HG
Tel: 0115-911 6500
Fax: 0115-911 6501/6502

Investment Management Association (IMA)
65 Kingsway
London WC2B 6TD
Tel: 020-7831 0898
Unit Trust Information Service:
Tel: 020-8207 1361
Fax: 020-7831 9975
Website: www.investmentuk.org
The IMA publishes a free guide to investing on behalf of children through unit trusts and other investment funds which is available from the IMA website or by calling the Unit Trust Information Service

JourneyWise
Tel: (0870) 876 6969
Website: www.journeywise.co.uk

Kids' Clubs Network
Bellerive House
3 Muirfield Crescent
London E14 9SZ
Tel: 020-7512 2112
Helpline: 020-7512 2100
Email:
information.office@kidsclubs.org.uk
Website: www.kidsclubs.org.uk
Provides free general advice about out-of-school childcare and has a database of out-of-school clubs throughout the UK with details of location, opening hours and fees

LawNet
1st Floor
93-95 Bedford Street
Royal Leamington Spa
Warwickshire CV32 5BB
Tel: (01926) 886990
Fax: (01926) 886553
Email: admin@lawnet.co.uk
Website: www.lawnet.co.uk
Provides names and addresses of solicitors

Law Society of England and Wales
113 Chancery Lane
London WC2A 1PL
Tel: 020-7242 1222
Email:
info.services@lawsociety.org.uk
Website: www.lawsociety.org.uk
Provides names and addresses of solicitors

Law Society of Northern Ireland
Law Society House
90 Victoria Street
Belfast BT1 3JZ
Tel: 028-9023 1614
Fax: 028-9023 2606
Email: info@lawsoc-ni.org
Website: www.lawsoc-ni.org
Provides names and addresses of solicitors

Law Society of Scotland
26 Drumsheugh Gardens
Edinburgh EH3 7YR
Tel: 0131-226 7411
Fax: 0131-225 2934
Email: lawscot@lawscot.org.uk
Website: www.lawscot.org.uk
Provides names and addresses of solicitors

Leading Edge
Tel: (01892) 836622
Website: www.leadedge.co.uk

Legal Services Commission
85 Gray's Inn Road
London WC1X 8TX
Tel: 020-7759 0000
Website: www.legalservices.gov.uk

Lloyds TSB Scotland
Tel: (0800) 056 0156
Website: www.lloydstsb.com

London & Country Mortgages
Tel: (0800) 953 0304
Website: www.lcplc.co.uk

Manchester Building Society
Tel: (08709) 900800
Website: www.themanchester.co.uk

Mediation Northern Ireland
10 Upper Crescent
Belfast BT7 1NT
Tel: 028-9043 8614
Fax: 028-9031 4430
Email:
info@mediationnorthernireland.org
Website:
www.mediationnorthernireland.org

Money£acts
Moneyfacts Group plc
Moneyfacts House
66-70 Thorpe Road
Norwich NR1 1BJ
Tel: (0870) 225 0100
Fax: (0870) 225 0477
Email: enquiries@moneyfacts.co.uk
Website: www.moneyfacts.co.uk

Money£acts Life and Pensions
See *Money£acts*

MoneyGram
Tel: (0800) 018 0104
Website: www.moneygram.com

Music Masters and Mistresses Association
MMA Awards Book
Wayfaring
Smithers Lane
East Peckham
Tonbridge TN12 5HT
Email: mma.admin@cwcom.net
Website: www.mma-online.org.uk

Nannytax
PO Box 988
Brighton BN2 1BY
Tel: (01273) 626256
Fax: (01273) 607733
Email: mailbox@nannytax.co.uk
Website: www.nannytax.co.uk
Specialist payroll service for people who employ a nanny

National Childbirth Trust
Alexandra House
Oldham Terrace
Acton
London W3 6NH
Tel: (0870) 444 8707
Website:
www.nctpregnancyandbabycare.com

National Childminding Association
8 Masons Hill
Bromley
Kent BR2 9EY
Information line: (0800) 169 4486
(10am–4pm weekdays)
Website: www.ncma.org.uk
*Provides general advice about issues
relating to childminding*

**National Council for One Parent
Families**
255 Kentish Town Road
London NW5 2LX
Tel: 020-7428 5400
Helpline: (0800) 018 5026
Fax: 020-7482 4851
Email:
info@oneparentfamilies.org.uk
Website:
www.oneparentfamilies.org.uk
*Information for people bringing up
children on their own, together with advice
on maintenance, benefits and other money
matters*

National Minimum Wage Helpline
Tel: (0845) 600 0678
Website: www.tiger.gov.uk

National Savings & Investments
Tel: (0845) 964 5000
Email:
customerenquiries@nsandi.com
Website: www.nsandi.com

National Union of Students
Nelson Mandela House
461 Holloway Road
London N7 6LZ
Tel: 020-7272 8900
Fax: 020-7263 5713
Email: nusuk@nus.org.uk
Website: www.nusonline.co.uk

Nationwide Building Society
Tel: (0800) 302 010
Website: www.nationwide.co.uk

NatWest Mortgage Services
Tel: (0800) 400 999
Website: www.natwest.com

New Deal for Lone Parents Helpline
Tel: (0800) 868 868
Website: www.newdeal.gov.uk

New Tax Credits Helpline
Tel: (0845) 300 3900 (England,
Scotland and Wales);
(0845) 603 2000 (Northern Ireland)
*The specialist helpline for detailed
information about tax credits – to check
eligibility for the Child Tax Credit, the
Childcare Tax Credit and the Working
Tax Credit, use the New Tax Credits'
Information Line or website as detailed
below instead*

**New Tax Credits Information Line
and website**
Tel: (0800) 500 222
Website:
www.taxcredits.inlandrevenue.gov.uk
*To check your eligibility and/or get a claim
form (or claim online) for the Child Tax
Credit, the Childcare Tax Credit and the
Working Tax Credit*

NHS Student Grants Unit
22 Plymouth Road
Blackpool
Lancashire FY3 7JS
Tel: (01253) 655655
*For details of NHS bursaries in England
for students training to be healthcare
professionals*

NHS (Wales) Student Awards Unit
2nd Floor
Golate House
101 St Mary's Street
Cardiff CF10 1DX
Tel: 029-2026 1495
For details of NHS bursaries in Wales for
students training to be healthcare
professionals

Northern Ireland Co-ownership
Housing Association
Tel: (0800) 333 644
Email: nicha@co-ownership.org
Website: www.co-ownership.org

Norwich & Peterborough Building
Society
Tel: (01733) 362636
Website: www.npbs.co.uk

The Nuffield Foundation
28 Bedford Square
London
WC1B 3JS
Tel: 020-7631 0566
Fax: 020-7323 4877
Email: enef@nuffieldfoundation.org
Website:
www.nuffieldfoundation.org
For details of grants from the Elizabeth
Nuffield Educational Fund for the
childcare costs of student mothers

Office for Standards in Education
(OFSTED)
Alexandra House
33 Kingsway
London WC2B 6SE
Tel: 020-7421 6800
Helpline: (0845) 601 4771 (for
registration queries)
Helpline: (0845) 601 4772 (for
complaints and concerns)
Website: www.ofsted.gov.uk

Options Insurance
Tel: (0870) 876 7878
Website:
www.optionsinsurance.co.uk

Parents At Work
1–3 Berry Street
London EC1V 0AA
Tel: 020-7253 7243
Fax: 020-7253 6253
Email: info@parentsatwork.org.uk
Website: www.parentsatwork.org.uk
For information on all forms of childcare
options and sample contract of employment
for nannies, for which there is a small
charge (£5 in March 2003)

The Pension Service
Pension Guide
Orderline: (0845) 731 3233
Website: www.pensionguide.gov.uk

Professional Association of Nursery
Nurses (PANN)
2 St James Court
Friars Gate
Derby DE1 1BT
Tel: (01332) 372337
Email: pann@pat.org.uk

Royal Bank of Scotland
Tel: (0800) 917 3025
Website: www.rbs.co.uk

Saxon Insurance
Tel: (0871) 230 5000
Website: www.saxoninsurance.com

Scholarship Search UK
Website: www.scholarship-
search.org.uk

Scottish Federation of Housing Associations
38 York Place
Edinburgh EH1 3HU
Tel: 0131-556 5777
Fax: 0131-557 6028
Email: sfha@sfha.co.uk
Website: www.sfha.co.uk

Scottish Widows Bank
Tel: (0845) 608 0371
Website: www.scottishwidows.co.uk

Self Assessment Orderline
PO Box 37
St Austell PL25 5YN
Tel: (0845) 900 0404
Fax: (0845) 900 0604
Email: saorderline.ir@gtnet.gov.uk

Service Children's Education (UK)
Trenchard Lines
Upavon
Pewsey
Wiltshire SN9 6BE
Tel: (01980) 618244
Fax: (01980) 618245
Email: mod.sce.uk@gtnet.gov.uk
Website: www.sceschools.com

SFIA
Tel: (0845) 458 3690
Fax: (0845) 458 3691
Email: enquiries@sfia.co.uk
Website: www.sfia.co.uk
Independent financial advisers specialising in planning for school fees

Shared Ownership Advice Line
Tel: 020-7393 2000

Society of Financial Advisers (SOFA)
20 Aldermanbury
London EC2V 7HY
Tel: 020-7417 4410
Fax: 020-7600 0766
Email: info@sofa.org
Website: www.sofa.org
To find an independent financial adviser

Society of Trust and Estate Practitioners
26 Dover Street
London W1S 4LY
Tel: 020-7763 7152
Fax: 020-7763 7252
Email: step@step.org
Website: www.step.org
To find a solicitor who specialises in trusts and estates

Solicitors Family Law Association
PO Box 302
Orpington
Kent BR6 8QX
Tel: (01689) 850227
Fax: (01689) 855833
Email: sfla@btinternet.com
Website: www.sfla.org.uk

Standard Life Bank
Tel: (0845) 845 8450
Website: www.standardlifebank.com

State Boarding Information Service (STABIS)
Tel: (01325) 391272
Website: www.stabis.org.uk
To download a copy of the free booklet 'Parents' Guide to Maintained Boarding Schools' and obtain information on state boarding schools

Student Awards Agency for Scotland
Gyleview House
3 Redheughs Rigg
Edinburgh EH12 9HH
Tel: (0845) 111 1711
Fax: 0131-244 5887
Email: saas.geu@scotland.gsi.gov.uk
Website: www.saas.gov.uk

Student Loans Company
100 Bothwell Street
Glasgow G2 7JD
Tel: (0800) 405 010
Fax: 0141-306 2005
Website: www.slc.co.uk

Student Support Branch
Department for Employment and
Learning
Room 407, 4th Floor
39-49 Adelaide Street
Belfast BT2 8FD
Tel: 028-9025 7710
Fax: 028-9025 7747
Email: studentsupport@delni.gov.uk
Website:
www.delni.gov.uk/studentsupport

Student Support Information Line
Tel: (0800) 731 9133

**Student Support Sponsorship
Funding Directory**
CRAC/Hobsons
Customer Services
Plymbridge Distributors Ltd
Estover Road
Plymouth PL6 7PZ
Tel: (01752) 202301
Fax: (01752) 202331
Email: cserve@plymbridge.com

**Tailored Interactive Guidance on
Employment Rights**
Website: www.tiger.co.uk
*For advice on the national minimum
wage*

Teaching Information Line
Tel: (0845) 600 0991

Travel Advice Unit
Consular Directorate
Foreign & Commonwealth Office
Old Admiralty Building
London SW1A 2PA
Tel: (0870) 606 0290
Fax: 020-7008 0155
Email: consular.fco@gtnet.gov.uk
Website: www.fco.gov.uk
*For travel advice and information on
problems affecting safety in over 200
countries around the world*

Travel Insurance Club
Tel: (01702) 423398
Website: www.ticdirect.co.uk

UK College of Family Mediators
Alexander House
Telephone Avenue
Bristol BS1 4BS
Tel: 0117-904 7223
Fax: 0117-904 3331
Email: ukcfm@btclick.com
Website: www.ukcfm.co.uk

**Universities & Colleges Admissions
Service (UCAS)**
Rosehill
New Barn Lane
Cheltenham
Gloucestershire GL52 3LZ
Tel: (01242) 222444
Email: enquiries@ucas.ac.uk
Website: www.ucas.ac.uk

Welsh Assembly Government
Housing Division
Cardiff Bay
Cardiff CF10 3NQ
Tel: 029-2082 5111

Welsh Language Teaching
Information Line
Tel: (0845) 600 0992

Western Union
Tel: (0800) 833 833
Website: www.westernunion.com

Which? Books
Freepost
PO Box 44
Hertford SG14 1SH
Tel: (0800) 252100
Email: books@which.net
Website: www.which.net

Which? Magazine
Freepost
PO Box 44
Hertford SG14 1SH
Tel: (0800) 252100
Website: www.which.net

Worldwide Volunteering
7 North Street Workshops
Stoke sub Hamdon
Somerset TA14 6QR
Tel: (01935) 825588
Fax: (01935) 825775
Email: worldvol@worldvol.co.uk
Website:
www.worldwidevolunteering.org.uk

The Year Out Group
Queensfield
28 Kings Road
Easterton
Wiltshire SN10 4PX
Tel: (07980) 395789
Email: info@yearoutgroup.org
Website: www.yearoutgroup.org

Yorkshire Building Society
Tel: (0845) 120 0899
Website: www.ybs.co.uk

Index

ACAS helpline 43
accumulation-and-maintenance
    trusts 158, 160–1
adopted children 11, 16
    Statutory Adoption Pay 45–6,
        51, 56
    Statutory Paternity Pay 45–6
    Sure Start Maternity Grant
        43
Advisory Centre for Education
    90
after-school clubs 68, 72, 83
Aided Pupils' Scheme for
    Music and Dance 89
Assembly Learning Grant
    (Wales) 107
Attendance Allowance 60, 76
au pairs 69, 73, 82
    pay 69, 82
    visas 82

baby kit costs 8, 42
banks
    interest-free overdrafts 99,
        108
    third party mandate 119
    will-writing services 19
    youth accounts 142–3

bare trusts 158, 159–60, 164,
    166
bereaved parents
    Bereavement Allowance 65
    Bereavement Payment 65
    unmarried partners 64
    Widowed Parent's Allowance
        65
Boarding Schools Association
    88
building-society accounts 141
business property relief 176

capital gains tax
    children and 144, 146
    on gifts 170–1, 177
    trusts and 164–5, 169
Care Leavers' Grant 106
charitable help
    private schooling 89–90
    student mothers 78
    university fees 107–8
Child Benefit 8, 47–9, 129
    backdated claims 47
    Child Benefit (Lone Parent)
        rate 47
    claiming 47–8
    duration of payments 48

eligibility for 47
payment periods 47
value 47
child maintenance 51, 62–4
    CSA assessments 62–3
    tax credits and 64
    value 63–4
Child Support Agency 62
Child Tax Credit 8, 43, 46,
        49–55
    assessing household income
        50–1
    baby element 44, 46, 54
    backdated claims 55, 61
    and disabled children 52, 55
    disabled parents 60
    duration of 49
    eligibility for 49, 130–1
    higher rates 46, 55, 56, 130
    Inland Revenue penalties 53,
        55
    non-working parents 51–2, 54
    qualifying for 46
    state benefits and 50, 51
    value 49, 51–2, 54
    when to claim 53, 55, 61
Child Trust Fund 136, 157
childcare
    after-school childcare 68, 72,
        83
    au pairs 69, 73, 82
    childminders 68, 72
    day nurseries 67, 68
    holiday arrangements 67, 83
    nannies 69, 79–82
    private nursery schools 67
    registered and approved 72
    state nursery schools 67
    workplace nurseries 75–6

childcare costs 8, 42, 67–82, 131
    after-school clubs 68, 72, 83
    at home 69
    childminders 68
    guardians and 21, 22, 32
    holiday playschemes 68
    nannies 69, 81–2
    outside the home 67–9
childcare costs, help with 70–9
    disabled parents 76–7
    employer help 75–6
    four-year-olds 70–1
    Nursery Education Grant
        Scheme 70–1
    pre-school 47, 70–1
    student parents 77–9
    three-year-olds 71
    unemployed parents 79
    working parents 71–5
Childcare Grant 62, 77–9
ChildcareLink 70, 72
Childcare Tax Credit 8, 56,
        71–5, 76–7
    backdated claims 74
    disabled parents 76–7
    duration of payments 74
    eligibility 72–3, 73
    increases 74
    overpayments 75
    value 71–2, 73–4
    when to claim 74–5
childminders 68, 72
    Home Childcarers scheme 72
    registration 73
children and money 136–44
    parental influence 136,
        138–9, 140
    personal finance training 136,
        140

pocket money 137–8
savings accounts 140–2, 144
savings habit 138–43
tax 139, 143, 144, 146, 149,
    150, 154, 164
youth accounts 142–3
see also nest eggs
children and work 138–9
employment outside the
    home 138–9
legal restrictions 138–9
minimum age 138
tax treatment 139
Children and Young Persons
    Act 1933 138
Children's Bonus Bonds
    149–50
Children's Information Service
    (CIS) 70, 72
Children's Savings Bonds 149,
    150–1
Children's Tax Credit 61
backdated claims 61
value 61
see also Child Tax Credit
cohabiting parents
and bereavement 64
and intestacy 15
Northern Ireland 16
Scotland 17
Community Service Volunteers
    114
costs of bringing up children
    42–3, 128–35
baby kit 8, 42, 131
budgeting for 132–3
childcare 8, 42, 67–82, 131
feeding, clothing and
    entertainment 8, 42

further education 8–9,
    94–102, 109–12
saving up 7–8, 133–5
school fees 8, 42, 85–93
start-up costs 42–3
state help with 43–66
total costs 9, 42
Council Tax Benefit 60
credit cards, student-friendly
    108
critical illness insurance 29, 35

day nurseries 67, 68
Daycare Trust 67, 76
debts, paying off children's
    124–5
Department for Education and
    Skills 101, 103
Department for Work and
    Pensions 37
Disability Living Allowance 55,
    60, 76
Highest Care Component
    55, 60
disabled children
Child Tax Credit 52, 55
Home Childcarers scheme
    72
Home Responsibilities
    Protection and 48
insurance and 26
parental leave 43–4
trusts and 157, 166
wills and 18
disabled parents 46
Child Tax Credit 60
childcare costs 76–7
Childcare Tax Credit 72, 76–7
Working Tax Credit 58, 60

Disabled Students' Allowance 105

disabled students, help with university fees 105–6

discretionary trusts 159, 161–2, 165, 166, 178

District Probate Registry 20

divorce
child maintenance 62
legal advice 62
mediation 62

Early Years' Grant *see* Nursery Education Grant Scheme

education *see* schooling; university education

Education Maintenance Allowance 85

Education Otherwise 90

educational charities 89–90

Elizabeth Nuffield Educational Fund 78

emergency time off 75, 76

employment
career breaks 33, 134
children 138–9
emergency time off 75, 76
flexible working rights 75
help with childcare costs 75–6
high-risk occupations 28, 39
parental leave 43–4, 75, 134
sick pay schemes 33, 37
student loan clearance 98

estate
division of, on intestacy 15–16
estate spreading 177

family protection *see* life insurance

family-income benefit insurance policies 22–3, 24, 26, 27, 28–9

flexible working rights 75

foster carers, taxation of income 66

Friendly Society savings plans 154

further education *see* university education

gap year 113–20
cost 113
emergency cash 119–20
funding 113, 115–16
gap-year companies 115
grants 116
insurance 116–19
medical emergencies and repatriation 117
options 114–15
parental support 113
power of attorney 119
risky pursuits 118

Gift Aid scheme 51

gifts
capital gains tax 170–1, 177
chargeable transfers 162
for education, training or maintenance 171
inheritance tax 170–80
lifetime gifts 171–2, 177
potentially exempt transfers 172
regular gifts 171
with reservation 177
small gifts 171, 180

tax on 170–80
tax-bearing gifts 174
tax-free gifts 171–2, 177
to spouses 173
to trusts 162, 165–6
wedding gifts 172
Graduate Endowment
(Scotland) 95
grandparents
and money gifts 9, 149
and trusts 156, 157, 158, 160,
161
grants
gap year 116
university education 61–2,
105, 106–7
Grants Register 108
guardians
appointing 11, 12, 13, 14, 16,
19
and childcare costs 21, 22, 32
Guardian's Allowance 51,
65–6
state help for 65–6

holiday playschemes 68
home
inheritance and 16
joint tenancy 15, 16, 179
making a gift of 177
moving 131–2
tenancy in common 15, 16,
179
see also property purchase
Home Childcarers scheme 72
Home Responsibilities
Protection 48–9
housing associations 127
Housing Benefit 60

Incapacity Benefit 37, 45, 51, 60
income, falling, coping with
128–31
Income Support 43, 60, 63
disability premium 60
income tax, trusts and 156, 164,
165, 169
income-protection insurance 7,
29, 33–41
'activities of daily working'
36
age and 39
automatic increases in cover
37
budget policies 35
costs 39–41, 43
cover calculation 37–9
cover options 36–7
deferred period 38, 40
duration 34
employer provision 33
gender and 39
guaranteed 34
houseperson cover 34, 37
occupational groups 39
proportionate benefit 36
rehabilitation benefit 36
renewable 35
reviewable 34
'unable to work' definition
36
Independent Financial Advisers
(IFAs) 29, 40, 93, 148, 166,
167
Independent Schools Council
information service (ISCis)
86, 87
Individual Savings Accounts
(ISAs) 51, 111, 144

Industrial Injuries Disablement
    Benefit 60, 76
inflation
    inflation-linked insurance 24
    university fees and 112
inheritance *see* inheritance tax;
    intestacy; wills
inheritance tax 12
    business property relief 176
    calculation 173–4
    chargeable transfers 162
    on death 172–4
    gifts and 148, 170–80
    insurance policy proceeds 31,
        173
    nest eggs and 148
    nil-rate band 173, 178
    planning for 174–80
    rates 162, 171
    seven-year rule 166, 172, 174,
        177
    trusts and 156, 162, 163,
        165–6
insurance
    critical illness insurance 29, 35
    gap year 116–19
    house contents 100
    income-protection insurance
        7, 29, 33–41
    mortgage-payment-
        protection insurance 35
    payment-protection
        insurance 35
    student insurance 100–1
    see also life insurance
interest-in-possession trusts
    159, 162–4
intestacy 14–17, 178
    children and 15, 16

cohabiting parents 15
and deed of variation 17
division of the estate 15–16
lone parents 15–16
married parents 15
Northern Ireland 16
Scotland 16–17
Invalid Vehicle Scheme 60, 76
investment trusts 153, 154
investments
    cash-based 111, 145, 148–51
    for children 147–55
    designating for a child 146–7,
        153, 159
    equity-based 111, 148, 152–5
    financial advice 148
    nest eggs 145–55
    tax treatment 149, 150, 154

Jobseeker's Allowance, income-
    based 43, 63

Kids' Club Network 72

Law Society 18, 167, 180
Legal Help 18
life insurance 7, 21–32
    before baby's birth 21
    calculation 25–6
    cheapest deals 175
    costs 27–30, 43
    critical illness cover 29
    gender and 28
    inflation-linked policies 24
    inheritance tax and 31, 173
    investment element 175
    joint-life policies 175
    life-of-another policy 31
    occupational groups 28

sum insured 25, 27
term insurance 21–5, 175
updating 21
whole-life insurance 23, 175
writing a policy in trust 20,
    31–2, 174–5
lone parents
Child Benefit 47
child maintenance 62–4
childcare costs 79
Childcare Tax Credit 72
and guardianship 13, 16
income-protection insurance
    7, 33
intestacy 15
New Deal for Lone Parents
    79
Northern Ireland 16
Scotland 17
and tax credits 55, 56, 57, 72
wills 15–16, 18
Working Tax Credit 56, 57

maternity pay 44–5, 128–9
Maternity Allowance 44–5,
    51, 56, 128
Statutory Maternity Pay 44,
    45, 51, 128, 129
medical and dental students 107
mobile phone bills 109
mortgages
100 per cent mortgages 122,
    126
affordability, assessing 124–5
flexible mortgages 91, 110
graduate mortgages 126
guarantors 126
high lending fees 122, 125
increasing 127, 132

interest rates 122
mortgage indemnity
    guarantee 122
mortgage-payment-protection
    insurance 35
repayment mortgages 23
size of loan 121–2

nannies 69, 79–82
au pairs 69, 73, 82
childminder registration 73
contract of employment 80
daily nannies 69, 81
employer duties 79–80
live-in nannies 69
minimum wage rules 81–2
nanny agencies 79
nanny-sharing 69
pay 69, 81–2
tax and NI 80–1
National Childminding
    Association 73
National Insurance
and Home Responsibilities
    Protection 48
school-age workers 139
voluntary contributions 48,
    98, 155
National Minimum Wage 81–2
National Savings & Investment
    accounts 142
nest eggs 145–55
designating for a child 146–7,
    159
earmarking own savings
    148
inheritance tax and 148
investing in the child's name
    145–6, 148, 152–3

investment choice 147–55
tax and 146
New Deal for Lone Parents 79
new parents
start-up costs 42–3
state help 43
Sure Start Maternity Grant 43
New Tax Credits Helpline 54,
56
Northern Ireland
intestacy 16
shared ownership schemes
127
Nursery Education Grant
Scheme 70–1, 78
nursery schools 67, 68

open-ended investment
companies (OEICs) 153,
154
orphaned children 11, 13
out-of-hours clubs 68, 72, 83

parental responsibility 13, 14,
16
Parents At Work 80
Parent's Learning Allowance
46, 61–2
paternity leave and pay 45–6,
134
pensions
Basic State Pension 48, 155
Home Responsibilities
Protection 48–9
personal pensions 51
stakeholder pensions 51,
154–5
War Disablement Pension 60,
76

pester power 137
pocket money 137–8
levels of 137–8
pay rises 137
power of attorney 119
power-of-appointment trusts
see interest-in-possession
trusts
pre-school provision
childcare costs 67, 68
free places 47, 70–1
Premium Bonds 151
private schools 85–93
bursaries 88
charitable help 89–90
choir schools 89
fees 8, 42, 85–93
foundation awards 89
help with costs 87–90
league tables 87
music scholarships 89
scholarships 88, 89
Service Children's Education
88
special groups 89
private schools (fees) 8, 42,
85–93
affinity card system 91
borrowing to pay 91
composition fee schemes 93
monthly direct debit
payments 91
planning for 90–3
pre-payment 93
school fee plans 92
Professional Association of
Nursery Nurses 80
property purchase 121–7
deposits 122, 123, 125

designated disadvantaged
  areas 124
joint purchase 126–7
parental help 124–7
shared ownership schemes
  127
stamp duty 124
upfront costs 122, 123, 125
see also mortgages

Retail Prices Index (RPI) 112

savings accounts
building-society accounts 141
cash cards 142
for children 140–2, 144
designated accounts 159
National Savings &
  Investment accounts 142
for paying tax before probate
  175–6
perks 140
regular-savings accounts 125
Scholarship Search UK 108
schooling 83–93
after-school childcare 68, 72,
  83
home education 90
school meals, free 84
school transport policies 84
see also pre-school provision;
  private schools; state
  schools
Scotland
intestacy 16–17
shared ownership schemes
  127
trusts 162
university education 95

self-employment, income-
  protection insurance 34, 37
Service Children's Education 88
Severe Disablement Allowance
  60
share-based investments 152–5
for children 152–5
in the child's name 152–3
collective investments 153–4
designated holdings 153
Friendly Society savings
  plans 154
investment trusts 153, 154
open-ended investment
  companies (OEICs) 153,
  154
stakeholder pensions 154–5
unit trusts 153, 154
Society of Financial Advisers 29
Society of Trust and Estate
  Practitioners 18
solicitors
divorce advice 62
house buying and 123
trusts and 166–7, 180
wills and 17–18, 179, 180
stakeholder pensions 154–5
stamp duty 124
state benefits
Benefit Enquiry Line 37
and Child Tax Credit 50, 51
see also individual benefits
State Boarding Information
  Service (STABIS) 88
state schools
boarding schools 88
catchment areas 85
Education Maintenance
  Allowance 85

extra tuition costs 83
free school meals 84
free transport 84
incidental expenses 8, 83, 84
low-income families 84–5
uniform allowance 84
voluntary donations 83
Statutory Adoption Pay 45–6,
    51, 56
Statutory Maternity Pay 44, 45,
    51, 56, 128, 129
Statutory Paternity Pay 45–6, 56
Statutory Sick Pay 37, 38, 56
stepchildren 16
student loans 8, 9, 102–4
    and credit records 104
    debt clearance 98
    government help with
        repayment 98, 106
    interest payable 98, 102
    minimum and maximum
        loans 102–3
    repayment 103–4
    teacher trainees 98, 106
    written-off loans 98
Student Loans Company 9, 102
student parents
    charitable help 78
    Child Tax Credit 49, 54
    childcare costs 77–9
    Childcare Grant 62, 77–9
    Parent's Learning Allowance
        46, 61–2
Student Support Information
    Line 101
Student Support Sponsorship
    Funding Directory 108
students
    average student expenditure 99

bank overdrafts and credit
    cards 108
disabled students 105–6
formerly in care 106
from low-income
    households 107
independent students 9, 95
medical and dental students
    107
mobile phone bills 109
trainee teachers 98, 106–7
see also student loans; student
    parents
Sure Start Maternity Grant 43

Tailored Interactive Guidance
    on Employment Rights
    (TIGER) 43
tax
    children and 139, 143, 144,
        146, 149, 150, 154, 164
    nannies 80–1
    nest eggs 146
    school-age workers 139
    see also capital gains tax;
        income tax; inheritance
        tax
tax allowances, child 144, 146
tax credits
    entitlement 130
    and maintenance payments
        64
    value for working parents 56,
        57, 58–9
    see also Child Tax Credit;
        Children's Tax Credit;
        Working Tax Credit
tax rebates 130
tax-avoidance schemes 177

teachers
  bursaries and grants 106–7
  shortage subjects 106
  student loan clearance 98,
    106
  trainees 106–7
tenancies
  joint tenancy 15, 16, 179
  tenancy in common 15, 16,
    179
term insurance 21–5, 175
  cash-back policies 22
  decreasing term 23, 24
  family-income benefit
    policies 22–3, 24, 26, 27,
    28–9
  increasing term 23
  joint-life policies 24–5
  level term 23
  lump-sum policies 22, 24,
    26–7, 30
Travel Advice Unit 117
trusts 9, 14–15, 156–69, 178
  accumulation-and-
    maintenance trusts 158,
    160–1
  bare trusts 158, 159–60, 164,
    166
  beneficiaries 158, 162–3,
    167–8
  capital beneficiaries 162–3
  capital gains tax and 164–5,
    169
  Child Trust Fund 136, 157
  discretionary trusts 159,
    161–2, 165, 166, 178
  gifts to 162, 165–6
  income tax and 156, 164, 165,
    169

inheritance tax and 156, 162,
    163, 165–6
  interest-in-possession trusts
    159, 162–4
  legal advice 166–7
  life tenants 162, 164
  ready-made trusts 166
  reasons for 156–7
  reclaiming tax 165
  reversionary interest 162–3
  setting up 166–9
  settlors 158
  trust deeds 161, 166, 167
  trustees 14, 19, 158, 167–9
  will trusts 15, 17, 162, 163
  writing an insurance policy
    in trust 20, 31–2, 175–6
tutors 83

unemployed parents
  Child Tax Credit 49
  childcare costs 79
uniform allowance 84
unit trusts 153, 154
university education 94–112
  costs 8–9, 94–102, 109–12
  in Scotland 95
  student insurance 100–1
  in Wales 105, 106, 107
  see also students; university
    fees
university fees 8–9, 94–102,
    109–12
  Access to Learning Fund 105
  Care Leavers' Grant 106
  charitable help 107–8
  disabled students 105–6
  grants 61–2, 105, 106–7
  Hardship Funds 105

investment plans 111
money shortfall 99
parental borrowing to pay 110
parental contribution 8–9,
    94–5, 97, 100, 102,
    109–12
parental income assessment
    95–6
parental income, payment
    out of 109
savings plans 111–12
tuition fees 9, 94, 101
see also student loans

volunteer work 114–15

Wales
    shared ownership schemes
        127
    students 105, 106, 107
War Disablement Pension 60,
    76
wedding gifts 172
whole life insurance 23, 175
Widowed Parent's Allowance
    65
wills 7, 11–20, 178
    bank will-writing services 19
    deed of variation 17, 179–80
    drawing up 17–20

executors 18–19
guardianship provisions 11,
    14, 19
intestacy 14–17, 178
legal assistance 17–18
legal charges 18, 42
marriage/remarriage and 12
matters covered 20
necessity for 11–12
safekeeping 20
setting up trusts 15, 17, 162,
    163
updating 12
witnesses 20
Working Tax Credit 33, 46, 51,
    55–61
    assessment of household
        income 55
    backdated claims 61
    childcare element *see*
        Childcare Tax Credit
    disability element 58, 60
    eligibility 56
    when to claim 61
workplace nurseries 75–6
Worldwide Volunteering 115

Year Out Group 115, 116
Young Volunteer Challenge
    scheme 114

The Which? Guide to Living Together

The number of couples cohabiting in preference to marrying is increasing rapidly. Even if their relationship is long term and similar in many respects to marriage, unmarried couples, both heterosexual and same-sex, should be aware that the law treats them differently from those who are married.

The Which? Guide to Living Together explodes the myth of the 'common law wife', pointing out that irrespective of the length of the relationship, an unmarried woman does not have the same rights in law as a married one. The book shows you how to protect your financial and legal rights while in a relationship – including how to draw up a cohabitation agreement – and tells you where you stand if you split up or if your partner dies. The issues of choice of surname for children, parental responsibility and adoption are discussed in detail. For couples in the process of breaking up, the sections on mediation and how to resolve disputes over children and property will be invaluable.

Packed with case histories and tips, and with sample agreements and useful forms, this guide explains how the law affects heterosexual and same-sex couples with respect to children, property, inheritance, pensions, company privileges and state benefits. Separate chapters deal with the differences in law in Scotland and Northern Ireland.

Paperback   216 x 135mm   192 pages   £9.99

Available from bookshops, and by post from
Which?, Dept BKLIST, Castlemead,
Gascoyne Way, Hertford X, SG14 1LH
or phone FREE on (0800) 252100
quoting Dept BKLIST and your credit card details

WHICH? BOOKS

The following is a selection of books on money matters from those published by Which? Books. For a full list of titles available please contact the address below

Be Your Own Financial Adviser	448 pages	£10.99
420 Legal Problems Solved	352 pages	£9.99
Life After Debt	224 pages	£6.99
160 Letters that Get Results	352 pages	£10.99
Make Your Own Will	28 pages	£10.99

Action Pack (A5 wallet with forms and 28-page booklet)

Rip Off Britain – and how to beat it	256 pages	£5.99
Take Control of Your Pension	48 pages	£10.99

Action Pack (A5 wallet with calculation sheets and 48-page booklet)

What to Do When Someone Dies	192 pages	£9.99
The Which? Guide to Baby Products	240 pages	£9.99
The Which? Guide to Doing Your Own Conveyancing	208 pages	£9.99
The Which? Guide to Employment	352 pages	£11.99
The Which? Guide to Giving and Inheriting	288 pages	£10.99
The Which? Guide to Help in the Home	208 pages	£9.99
The Which? Guide to Living Together	192 pages	£9.99
The Which? Guide to Money in Retirement	288 pages	£10.99
The Which? Guide to Money on the Internet	256 pages	£9.99
The Which? Guide to Planning Your Pension	368 pages	£10.99
The Which? Guide to Renting and Letting	352 pages	£11.99
Which? Way to Buy, Own and Sell a Flat	352 pages	£10.99
Which? Way to Buy, Sell and Move House	320 pages	£10.99
Which? Way to Save and Invest 2002-3	336 pages	£14.99
Which? Way to Save Tax 2002-3	242 pages	£14.99
Wills and Probate	192 pages	£10.99

Available from bookshops, and by post from
Which?, Dept BKLIST, Castlemead,
Gascoyne Way, Hertford X, SG14 1LH
or phone FREE on (0800) 252100
quoting Dept BKLIST and your credit card details